T0194773

An Analysis of

Natalie Zemon Davis's

The Return of Martin Guerre

Joseph Tendler

Published by Macat International Ltd
24:13 Coda Centre, 189 Munster Road, London SW6 6AW.

Distributed exclusively by Routledge
2 Park Square, Milton Park, Abingdon, Oxon OX14 4RN
711 Third Avenue, New York, NY 10017, USA

Routledge is an imprint of the Taylor & Francis Group, an informa business

www.macat.com
info@macat.com

Cataloguing in Publication Data
A catalogue record for this book is available from the British Library.
Library of Congress Cataloguing-in-Publication Data is available upon request.
Cover illustration:Capucine Deslouis

ISBN 978-1-912302-49-9 (hardback)
ISBN 978-1-912127-60-3 (paperback)
ISBN 978-1-912281-37-4 (e-book)

Notice
The information in this book is designed to orientate readers of the work under analysis,
to elucidate and contextualise its key ideas and themes, and to aid in the development
of critical thinking skills. It is not meant to be used, nor should it be used, as a
substitute for original thinking or in place of original writing or research. References and
notes are provided for informational purposes and their presence does not constitute
endorsement of the information or opinions therein. This book is presented solely for
educational purposes. It is sold on the understanding that the publisher is not engaged
to provide any scholarly advice. The publisher has made every effort to ensure that
this book is accurate and up-to-date, but makes no warranties or representations with
regard to the completeness or reliability of the information it contains. The information
and the opinions provided herein are not guaranteed or warranted to produce particular
results and may not be suitable for students of every ability. The publisher shall not be
liable for any loss, damage or disruption arising from any errors or omissions, or from
the use of this book, including, but not limited to, special, incidental, consequential or
other damages caused, or alleged to have been caused, directly or indirectly, by the
information contained within.

CONTENTS

THE MACAT LIBRARY

The Macat Library is a series of unique academic explorations of seminal works in the humanities and social sciences – books and papers that have had a significant and widely recognised impact on their disciplines. It has been created to serve as much more than just a summary of what lies between the covers of a great book. It illuminates and explores the influences on, ideas of, and impact of that book. Our goal is to offer a learning resource that encourages critical thinking and fosters a better, deeper understanding of important ideas.

Each publication is divided into three Sections: Influences, Ideas, and Impact. Each Section has four Modules. These explore every important facet of the work, and the responses to it.

This Section-Module structure makes a Macat Library book easy to use, but it has another important feature. Because each Macat book is written to the same format, it is possible (and encouraged!) to cross-reference multiple Macat books along the same lines of inquiry or research. This allows the reader to open up interesting interdisciplinary pathways.

To further aid your reading, lists of glossary terms and people mentioned are included at the end of this book (these are indicated by an asterisk [*] throughout) – as well as a list of works cited.

Macat has worked with the University of Cambridge to identify the elements of critical thinking and understand the ways in which six different skills combine to enable effective thinking.
Three allow us to fully understand a problem; three more give us the tools to solve it. Together, these six skills make up the **PACIER** model of critical thinking. They are:

ANALYSIS – understanding how an argument is built
EVALUATION – exploring the strengths and weaknesses of an argument
INTERPRETATION – understanding issues of meaning

CREATIVE THINKING – coming up with new ideas and fresh connections
PROBLEM-SOLVING – producing strong solutions
REASONING – creating strong arguments

To find out more, visit **WWW.MACAT.COM.**

CRITICAL THINKING AND
THE RETURN OF MARTIN GUERRE

Primary critical thinking skill: REASONING
Secondary critical thinking skill: INTERPRETATION

Few stories are more captivating than the one told by Natalie Zemon Davis in *The Return of Martin Guerre*. Basing her research on records of a bizarre court case that occurred in 16th-century France, she uses the tale of a missing soldier – whose disappearance threatens the livelihood of his peasant wife – to explore complex social issues. Davis takes rich material – dramatic enough to have been the basis of two major films – and uses it to explore issues of identity, women's role in peasant society, the interior lives of the poor, and the structure of village society, all of them topics that had previously proved difficult for historians to grapple with.

Davis displays fine qualities of reasoning throughout – not only in constructing her own narrative, but also in persuading her readers of her point of view. Her work is also a fine example of good interpretation – practically every document in the case needs to be assessed for issues of meaning.

ABOUT THE AUTHOR OF THE ORIGINAL WORK

The historian **Natalie Zemon Davis** was born in the US city of Detroit in 1928. She was educated privately in Michigan, eventually earning a PhD from the University of Michigan in 1950. Her Marxist political beliefs shaped her interest in recovering the histories of people overlooked by traditional studies in the discipline. But those beliefs also forced her from the US to Canada in the 1960s to find teaching work. From 1978 to 1996, Davis taught gender studies, social and Jewish history, and film at the University of California, Berkeley. She is a former president of the American Historical Association.

ABOUT THE AUTHOR OF THE ANALYSIS

Dr Joseph Tendler received his PhD from the University of St Andrews. He is the author of Opponents of the Annales School.

ABOUT MACAT

GREAT WORKS FOR CRITICAL THINKING

Macat is focused on making the ideas of the world's great thinkers accessible and comprehensible to everybody, everywhere, in ways that promote the development of enhanced critical thinking skills.

It works with leading academics from the world's top universities to produce new analyses that focus on the ideas and the impact of the most influential works ever written across a wide variety of academic disciplines. Each of the works that sit at the heart of its growing library is an enduring example of great thinking. But by setting them in context – and looking at the influences that shaped their authors, as well as the responses they provoked – Macat encourages readers to look at these classics and game-changers with fresh eyes. Readers learn to think, engage and challenge their ideas, rather than simply accepting them.

'Macat offers an amazing first-of-its-kind tool for interdisciplinary learning and research. Its focus on works that transformed their disciplines and its rigorous approach, drawing on the world's leading experts and educational institutions, opens up a world-class education to anyone.'

Andreas Schleicher,
Director for Education and Skills, Organisation for Economic
Co-operation and Development

'Macat is taking on some of the major challenges in university education … They have drawn together a strong team of active academics who are producing teaching materials that are novel in the breadth of their approach.'

Prof Lord Broers,
former Vice-Chancellor of the University of Cambridge

'The Macat vision is exceptionally exciting. It focuses upon new modes of learning which analyse and explain seminal texts which have profoundly influenced world thinking and so social and economic development. It promotes the kind of critical thinking which is essential for any society and economy. This is the learning of the future.'

Rt Hon Charles Clarke, former UK Secretary of State for Education

'The Macat analyses provide immediate access to the critical conversation surrounding the books that have shaped their respective discipline, which will make them an invaluable resource to all of those, students and teachers, working in the field.'

Professor William Tronzo, University of California at San Diego

WAYS IN TO THE TEXT

KEY POINTS

- Natalie Zemon Davis is a leading American historian of French, social, and cultural history,* a feminist and Marxist* whose life and work has been infused with her radical politics.

- *The Return of Martin Guerre* tells a new version of a mysterious and controversial sixteenth-century story that reads like a detective novel. Eight years after Martin Guerre disappears from a small French town, abandoning his wife and child, an imposter is taken to court for successfully assuming his identity—until the real Martin comes back.

- The book, associated in many readers' minds with the movie of the same name, combines extensive research and imaginative storytelling to bring a vanished world to life. It focuses on the role of women in peasant society, how members of the lower classes formed their identities, and how different cultures interacted. It is considered to be a major contribution to cultural history, although controversial for the way in which the author used her imagination to fill in some of the blanks in the historical record.

Who was Natalie Zemon Davis?

The daughter of Jewish* European immigrants, Natalie Zemon Davis was born in 1928 in Detroit, in the United States. As a girl she was drawn to the French language, which she studied at a private school in Michigan, where she grew up. She graduated from Smith College, a small but well-regarded liberal arts school in Massachusetts, and went on to earn a master's degree from Radcliffe College in 1950. She received her doctorate from the University of Michigan in 1959. The study of history, especially that of her own European ancestors, has fascinated Davis throughout her life.

In 1948 she married Chandler Davis,* a Canadian mathematician and author. Both of them believed in Marxism, the political ideology based on the philosophy that the struggle between social classes is a major force in history and that society should contain no class barriers. Davis's political views and activities shaped her work and drove her interest as a historian in the lives of ordinary people. Her beliefs fueled her interest in social reform, women's rights, economic and racial equality, and the protection of society's most vulnerable people.

In the 1960s, Davis and her husband moved to Canada because they could not get teaching jobs in America. This was at the height of a period in US history known as the McCarthy era,* when suspected communist* sympathizers—including Marxists like Davis and her husband—were under intense scrutiny. She finally landed a job teaching history at the University of Toronto, then moved to the University of California, Berkeley, before relocating to Princeton University, where she taught classes about gender, social and Jewish history, and film, from 1978 to 1996.

Now retired, Davis remains an active scholar. She has received major public awards for her work, including the 2012 National Humanities Medal, a US award for achievement in the study of social sciences. That same year she was named a Companion of the Order of Canada for her contributions to the study of human culture. In 1988 she became only the second female president of the American Historical Association,* the influential organization of historians.

What Does *The Return of Martin Guerre* Say?

The Return of Martin Guerre has three important themes. First, the book tells a once unknown story of French life that takes place during the early-modern* era of European history, the period from around 1500 to 1800. Davis reinterprets the tale of Martin Guerre, a peasant living in the French town of Artigat in the sixteenth century, who abandons his wife and child for eight years. After Guerre disappears, Arnaud du Tilh, a peasant from another part of France, arrives in Artigat and takes over Martin's life, becoming a believable impostor. Arnaud eventually gets caught for his crimes and Guerre returns to Artigat during the trial of the man who stole his identity. Davis shows that the past holds extraordinary and overlooked events and stories.

Second, in retelling this story Davis makes a new argument. She maintains that Martin Guerre's wife Bertrande plays a key role in helping Arnaud the imposter assume Martin's life. This conflicts with other versions of the tale that depict Bertrande as a passive victim of both Martin and Arnaud's behavior. Davis also examines how sixteenth-century peasants were able to reinvent their identities. In doing so, Davis explores in detail the way in which Arnaud takes over Martin's life. She looks at how Bertrande helps Arnaud create their fake marriage and cultivates her image in the town as the dutiful wife of the husband who has returned to her.

Third, Davis insists that one cannot understand historical events without putting them in context. Historians, she believes, need to borrow tools from other academic fields—particularly anthropology* (the study of human societies though observation of daily lives and customs) and ethnology* (the branch of anthropology that compares and contrasts different societies and tribes).

In *The Return of Martin Guerre*, Davis closely examines how people in Artigat interacted. For example, how does Bertrande use her community ties and her role in her family to support Arnaud's theft of Martin's identity? How does Protestantism,* a new religion in sixteenth-century France, help Bertrande and Arnaud create their fraudulent marriage? How do the judges at Arnaud's trial relate to him? The judges were men of noble birth, from the upper classes. So how do they view Arnaud, who is a rural peasant from a family of poor farmers, but a man with superior intellect?

Davis's challenge to historians of her era goes further, into an approach that drew criticism from her peers. Controversially, she uses her own imagination to fill in gaps in the story. She had access to many records, but there are parts of the tale that cannot be found in the archives. She urges other historians to follow her lead, in effect saying that it is acceptable to use a literary approach to history and to flesh out the narrative with educated assumptions and personal insights.

Yet, as a student in the 1950s, Davis had learned history as a science. Her professors taught her that, in order to write the most accurate historical accounts, it was necessary to research the records for hard evidence and facts. Such facts should be presented chronologically, as a sequence of events unfolding over time. From this point of view, only evidence verified through archival documents could make a story credible.

Davis has admitted that she did not find enough of this kind of evidence to justify her theory that Martin Guerre's wife played a key role in creating Arnaud's false identity. Davis uses her imagination, as a married woman, to suggest what Bertrande *must* have done under the circumstances. Because Davis had no proof of Bertrande's role— through records or documents—other historians criticized the book and the way in which Davis filled in some blanks. This was not history as a science, they argued: this was fiction.

Nevertheless, Davis's approach took hold, as historians expressed a growing interest in the work of literary scholars. Historians were no longer upholding the strict division between history as a science and history as literature and art. The book initiated a surge of interest among academics in the relationship between history and literature.

Why Does *The Return of Martin Guerre* Matter?

The Return of Martin Guerre matters in at least three distinct ways. First, the book fueled a renewed interest among historians in the lives of ordinary people, such as French peasants. The book was published in the early 1980s, just as American historians were changing their social, political, and intellectual views and becoming more curious about people from the lower classes of society. Together with Davis's unique focus on the role of women in the French peasant world of the sixteenth century, the book is important because it motivated other American historians to study new subjects. At the time of publication, women's studies and similar topics were relatively new offerings as college courses. Davis was particularly interested in the way relationships between men and women influenced past events, and how women used what power they had in the societies of their day.

Second, *The Return of Martin Guerre* underlines the importance of combining different fields of study with history. Davis draws from anthropology, ethnology, and literature to reconstruct the story of Martin Guerre. She places her account in the context of the sixteenth-century customs and beliefs of the town of Artigat in southern France

Third, Davis's work called more attention to the importance of history as a field of study. She decided to write the book while working as a historical consultant on a film about Martin Guerre, *Le Retour de Martin Guerre*,* released in 1982. Davis saw her 1983 book as an important complement to the film.

The Return of Martin Guerre asks readers to look at the relationship between the past and the present, which Davis sees as a conversation between then and now. She views this kind of work as shining a light on unknown cultures, and in doing so helping readers and students understand people from vastly different worlds. She considers that history is vital not only in understanding the past, but also in helping students and readers to become aware of other cultures. This might assist students, for example, in their studies abroad and be helpful to those interested in working for global organizations.

Finally, Davis's use of her imagination in telling the story of Martin Guerre encourages readers to use their own creativity in looking for solutions to problems. "

KEY QUESTIONS

Synthesize: What is Natalie Zemon Davis's reputation today?

Analyze: What themes and social issues arise from the story of Martin Guerre?

Apply: How can cultural history change the way its readers see the world?

SECTION 1
INFLUENCES

MODULE 1
THE AUTHOR AND THE HISTORICAL CONTEXT

KEY POINTS

- *The Return of Martin Guerre* is both a compelling story of truth and identity and a classic study in cultural history* that is still relevant today.

- Natalie Zemon Davis's commitment to cultural equality and diversity proved most important in shaping the book.

- The women's movement and the fight for civil rights had a big impact on the environment in which Davis worked.

Why Read this Text?

Published in 1983, *The Return of Martin Guerre* by Natalie Zemon Davis is worth reading for three main reasons. First, it is a strange and fascinating story of human relationships covering a wide range of topics including love, identity, fidelity, inheritance, law, class, and religion.

Second, it offers a radical way of looking at social and cultural history, combining sixteenth-century evidence with twentieth-century insights. "One of the most internationally influential of all American historians,"[1] Davis tries to understand past events based on extensive research of sources she found in archives across France. But she also puts forward ideas and views that go beyond those sources, thanks to her sweeping knowledge of peasant life in early-modern* France.

Third, Davis's work is key to understanding the nature of historical study today. In the 1980s *The Return of Martin Guerre* heralded a new wave of professional interest in social and cultural history. After the book was published, Davis's particular interests continued to push boundaries, championing gender history, using film as a historical

> ❝ I got very active in politics ... This political activity
> was very important for my work. It gave me a whole
> new way to look at revolutions and history in general. I
> had some excellent teachers at Smith, but none seemed
> to approach the big questions that fascinated me, about
> class and class conflict, about how the social world
> related to the intellectual world, about the big motors
> of historical change, and so on. ❞
>
> Rob Harding, "Interview with Natalie Zemon Davis

source, and studying the interactions of people from different
countries and cultures.

Author's Life

Like Arnaud du Tilh, one of the main characters in *The Return of
Martin Guerre*, Davis felt that she had lived life as an outsider in her
early years. She was Jewish and grew up in Detroit, attending the
private Kingswood School for girls.[2] Her love of French began when
she was young and she studied the language early in her schooling.[3]
Her European family background inspired her interest in European
history. She said in an interview that at the end of World War II,* "the
story of the concentration camps was being told; I had a special
connection with those pictures we would see in current events class."[4]

Davis also felt different because she was interested in radical causes
and ideas, including the left-wing political worldview of Marxism,*
world peace, racial equality, women's rights, and freedom of speech. All
of these passions fueled her contributions to public life,[5] primarily in
the field of history. She has written and co-edited 10 history books
and has produced many scholarly papers.

Davis's interests did not waver through college and graduate
school. At Smith College in Massachusetts, she developed as a historian

while becoming involved with a number of radical political causes and heading two groups dedicated to radical politics: "The Marxist Discussion Group" and "Young Progressives."[6] She further advanced her knowledge of French history in her graduate work at Harvard University and her doctoral studies at the University of Michigan.

Davis's early academic career took her across the United States and Canada. This was in the early 1950s—the era of McCarthyism*— when there was a widespread political crackdown on suspected communist* sympathizers.[7] The radical political views Davis shared with her husband Chandler Davis* at first made it hard for them to find work as teachers. However, she went on to teach at the University of Toronto, the University of California, Berkeley, and Princeton University.

While Davis was working as a historical consultant on the 1982 French film, *Le Retour de Martin Guerre,** she decided to write about the story on which the film was based. At the time she was the Henry Charles Lea Professor of History at Princeton, where she was also director of the Shelby Cullom Davis Center for Historical Studies.[8] By 1988, Davis was serving as president of the American Historical Association, the leading organization for professional historians across the globe.[9]

Author's Background

War and liberation shaped the era in which Davis lived. Although she was only a teenager during World War II, America's involvement in the conflict meant European events dominated the news. After the war ended, Davis campaigned against the 1948 Marshall Plan,* in which America gave massive financial aid to help rebuild Europe's shattered economies. Davis criticized the plan, believing it to be an American ploy to assert its global power, rather than a genuine act of financial assistance. "We protested the Marshall Plan," she said. "We wanted the aid to go through the United Nations* and not just be a means to expand American power."[10] Davis remained a critic of American foreign policy throughout her career.[11]

Davis was also involved in liberation movements and was particularly active in the student movement* of the 1960s. Although she was a professor, Davis joined with students across America to demand greater academic freedoms and a broader range of studies.[12] She played a public role in the Civil Rights Movement,* promoting the idea of equal opportunities for blacks and whites.[13] She also fought for equality for men and women, contributing to the women's liberation movement* of the 1960s and 1970s.[14]

Other causes that Davis was drawn to included rights for Hispanic immigrants in the US and rights for sexual minorities.[15] It was in this climate that Davis wanted to show that the underprivileged in society had always affected the course of history and that this knowledge could and should support equal rights for all people in modern-day America.[16]

NOTES

1   Philip Benedict, "Between Whig Traditions and New Histories: American Historical Writing about Reformation and Early Modern Europe," in *Imagined Histories: American Historians Interpret the Past*, ed. Anthony Molho and Gordon S. Wood (Princeton, NJ: Princeton University Press, 1998), 302.

2   Rob Harding, "Interview with Natalie Zemon Davis," in *Visions of History*, ed. Henry Abelove et al. (Manchester: Manchester University Press, 1983), 100–1.

3   Natalie Zemon Davis, *A Life of Learning* (New York: American Council of Learned Societies, 1997), 3, 5.

4   Harding, "Interview," 101.

5   Marnie Hughes-Warrington, "Natalie Zemon Davis," in *Fifty Key Thinkers on History* (London: Routledge, 2003), 56; Harding, "Interview," 102.

6   Harding, "Interview," 101.

7   Roger Adelson, "Interview with Natalie Zemon Davis," *Historian* 53 (1991): 408; Harding, "Interview," 104–5.

8 Davis, *Life of Learning*, 19.

9 Natalie Zemon Davis, "History's Two Bodies," *American Historical Review* 93 (1988): 1–2.

10 Harding, "Interview," 101.

11 Natalie Zemon Davis, *A Passion for History: Conversations with Denis Crouzet* (Kirksville, MO: Truman State University Press, 2010), 158–70.

12 Davis, *Life of Learning*, 13–14.

13 Harding, "Interview," 104.

14 Carla Hesse and Natalie Zemon Davis, "Why Gender and Women's Studies Matter," *Medievalists.net,* October 10, 2010, accessed April 23, 2015, http://www.medievalists.net/2010/10/10/natalie-zemon-davis-why-gender-and-womens-studies-matter/.

15 George Brown Tindall and David Emory Shi, *America: A Narrative History* (New York: W. W. Norton & Company, 2007), 972–82.

16 Georg G. Iggers, *Historiography in the Twentieth Century: From Scientific Objectivity to the Postmodern Challenge* (Middletown, CT: Wesleyan University Press, 1999), 101.

MODULE 2
ACADEMIC CONTEXT

KEY POINTS

- European history concerns itself with the study of Europe's past, whether particular local histories of a town or region or of a nation-state such as France or Ukraine.

- When *The Return of Martin Guerre* was published in the 1980s, European history was beginning to include cultural history.*

- Natalie Zemon Davis studied French history, examining its culture with a particular interest in gender relations, ordinary people, and popular beliefs.

The Work In Its Context

The Return of Martin Guerre played an important part in a new development in European history among American scholars. At the start of the twentieth century, historians like Natalie Zemon Davis were moving away from a focus on political and military history, both of which had been dominant themes up to that point. Progressive historians, scholars in a field called progressive or new history,* began to write about the importance of socio–economic aspects of European history and culture. Among them was James Harvey Robinson,* who shared Davis's views, saying: "When we consider the vast range of human interests, our histories furnish us with a sadly inadequate and misleading review of the past by ignoring so many areas of life."[1]

This approach was embraced by other well-known historians, including Charles Beard* and Arthur M. Schlesinger Jr.*[2] Students of these historians, perhaps most famous among them Daniel Boorstin,* continued the focus on progressive/new history, turning away from

> ❝ Increasingly in the 1970s and 1980s historians, not only in the West but in some cases also in the Eastern European countries, began to question the assumptions of social science history. ❞
>
> Georg G. Iggers, *Historiography in the Twentieth Century: From Scientific Objectivity to the Postmodern Challenge*

politics, diplomacy, religion, and military matters toward social, economic, and cultural issues.[3]

French history was also becoming a popular subject for American historians. French institutions and French journals had long been important in the training of American historians, but French and American scholars began to connect much more after France and America became allies in World War I and II.*

Overview of the Field

After 1970, Davis researched women and folk carnivals in France, in Languedoc and elsewhere, topics that feature heavily in *The Return of Martin Guerre*, before discovering the story of Martin Guerre in 1978. At this time European studies were changing under the influence of what is known as the "cultural turn."*[4] Starting in the 1970s among historians like Davis, the cultural turn describes a shift from the more scientific study of countries and large institutions to the stories and cultures of individuals. It provided a new focus on "the social process whereby people communicate meanings, make sense of their world, construct their identities, and define their beliefs and values."[5] Rather than view social relations as the result of fixed institutions and status, attention moved to how ordinary people made sense of their environment, how they shared conventions and codes with others, and how those cultural exchanges impacted on their behavior.

The cultural turn emerged alongside postmodernism,* a late

twentieth-century style of approaching history, the arts, and architecture. For historians, postmodernism created a "renewed emphasis on the experiences of concrete human beings"[6] among historians. An earlier generation of historians had tried to identify the stable and enduring structures that produced social order. So they had studied the role of the state, the Church, and the army in society; analyzing, for example, how the social, political, and religious elites molded the lives of everybody below them on the social ladder.

By contrast, postmodernists and cultural historians like Davis wanted to explore the world as it appeared to specific individuals. The people who interested them often came from the lower classes and oppressed groups. These historians had the "drive to amplify previously unheard voices from unprivileged groups and peoples; a preoccupation with gender as the most immediate generator of underprivileged or un-empowered status."[7] Davis believed each individual sees the world differently and she challenged scholars and the general public to rethink how events occurred—and who or what controlled them.[8]

Academic Influences

Davis had academic mentors who taught her to value both the careful study of facts and to explore the experiences of society's marginalized groups. Chief among them was literature professor Rosalie Colie,* who impressed Davis with the range of tools she borrowed from other fields.[9] This planted a seed in Davis's mind—that it was possible to write about history using the work of literary scholars as inspiration.

Davis was particularly drawn to the work of an American historian who specialized in British history, W. K. Jordan.* Like Davis, Jordan was fascinated by social history. As one of Davis's mentors, he helped her reach a higher level of achievement than most female scholars of her time. Jordan was "wedded to the notion that women should be able to make it,"[10] Davis said in an interview. Another of Davis's teachers, Palmer Throop,* pushed her to examine the role of women writers during the Renaissance,*[11] the period of European history between the fourteenth and seventeenth centuries that achieved significant progress in the sciences, arts, and literature.

Meanwhile, Davis's own reading and research was pointing her to France. She studied French history with what would become her hallmark approach—looking at events from a cultural and social perspective. Davis also encountered the work of Henri Hauser,* who had extensively researched the role of workers and printers during the Reformation,* the sixteenth-century religious movement in Europe that led to the establishment of the Protestant Church.[12]

From there, Davis discovered the work of two French historians, Marc Bloch* and Lucien Febvre,* both founders in 1929 of the journal *Annales* that pioneered an interdisciplinary approach to French history. Followers of the *Annales* school* supported combining social, economic, and cultural subjects, and Davis admired their approach. While still influenced by Marxism,* she chose to focus on the customs and beliefs of groups of peasants and other members of the lower classes.[13]

NOTES

1   James Harvey Robinson, "The New History," in *The New History: Essays Illustrating the Modern Historical Outlook* (New York: Macmillan, 1911), 2.

2   Ernst A. Breisach, *American Progressive History: An Experiment in Modernization* (Chicago: University of Chicago Press, 1993), 204.

3   Breisach, *Progressive History*, 11.

4   James W. Cook and Lawrence B. Glickman, "Twelve Propositions for a History of US Cultural History," in *The Cultural Turn in US History: Past, Present & Future*, ed. James W. Cook and Lawrence B. Glickman (Chicago: University of Chicago Press, 2008), 5–6.

5   Steven Best, "Cultural Turn," in *Blackwell Encyclopedia of Sociology*, ed. George Ritzer (Oxford: Blackwell, 2007), 177.

6   Georg G. Iggers, *Historiography in the Twentieth Century: From Scientific Objectivity to the Postmodern Challenge* (Middletown, CT: Wesleyan University Press, 1999), 97.

7   Michael Bentley, "Reflecting on the Modern Age," in *Companion to Historiography*, ed. Michael Bentley (London: Routledge, 1999), 489–90.

8   Rob Harding, "Interview with Natalie Zemon Davis," *Visions of History,* ed. Henry Abelove et al. (Manchester: Manchester University Press, 1983), 114.

9   *Medievalists.net*, "Interview with Natalie Zemon Davis," September 27, 2008, accessed April 23, 2015, http://www.medievalists.net/2008/09/27/interview-with-natalie-zemon-davis/.

10   Harding, "Interview," 103.

11   Natalie Zemon Davis, *A Life of Learning* (New York: American Council of Learned Societies, 1997), 7.

12   Harding, "Interview," 104.

13   Harding, "Interview," 103.

MODULE 3
THE PROBLEM

KEY POINTS

- Academics in the 1970s explored the role culture played in early-modern* European history.

- Emmanuel Le Roy Ladurie* identified institutions that shaped cultures, while Carlo Ginzburg* studied the worldview of an individual miller in sixteenth-century Italy.

- Natalie Zemon Davis combined these three approaches, and went a step further by examining the role of women in society.

Core Question

At the time that Natalie Zemon Davis published *The Return of Martin Guerre*, historians were beginning to question their approach. How could they also reconstruct the culture of past periods and peoples? The question was difficult to answer.

The consensus among historians from the late nineteenth century to the 1970s was that they should use scientific methods of studying the past, employing forensic tools, like a detective, to dig up and review historical documents and other evidence. "The professional historians of the late nineteenth century, in pursuit of the authority of science, consistently distanced themselves from, and disparaged, 'history as literature,' 'history as art.'"[1]

The problem arose because historians like Davis believed that factual sources could not tell the whole story, particularly about the lives of marginal groups who were less likely to have well-documented lives. Davis believed in using both archival materials and her own imagination to fill in the gaps where there were no records. As she

> ❝An event or practice (even a text) does not exist apart from the forces of the context that constitute it as what it is. Obviously, context is not merely background but the very conditions of possibility of something. It cannot be relegated to a series of footnotes or to an after-thought, to the first or last chapter. ❞
>
> Lawrence Grossberg, "Cultural Studies: What's In a Name (One More Time)"

recalled, "When I was a student, we were ordinarily taught as scientific historians to peel away the fictive elements in our documents so we could get at the real facts."[2]

The Participants

Those who supported the idea of history as a science claimed that their approach was the most credible because it was based on objective evidence. This belief in the need for evidence was generally shared among historians between the early 1940s and the early 1960s.[3] American historians borrowed from behavioral scientists (who studied human and animal behavior in a scientific way) to investigate population data and analyze social developments.[4]

Beyond America's shores, some members of the *Annales* school* in France were also supporting the use of newly available historical records. For example, by studying shipping data they made discoveries about the development of international trade, and then about social and cultural history.*[5]

While there was debate among scholars of the *Annales* school over whether scientific or cultural history was the most effective, there was growing acceptance of what was known as "progressive/new history." This approach to the subject was pioneered by American historians in the 1920s and emphasized the importance of researching the lives of ordinary people using both economic and social research. It connected

French and American historians, who had not paid much attention to each other's work until the 1970s.[6]

A friend of Davis's, Emmanuel Le Roy Ladurie, wrote a history of Languedoc, the home province in France of Arnaud du Tilh. Ladurie's book was published in French in 1966 and translated into English in 1974.[7] He wrote that the economic history of Languedoc showed successive periods of decline and growth in the early-modern era (from the end of the Middle Ages to around the 1500s). Languedoc never escaped this cycle because it was so conservative: peasants refused to accept modern methods of land management[8] and Languedoc's religious practices, its rule of law,* and social hierarchies remained largely unchanged.[9]

As Ladurie deepened his research, he focused on one particular village, Montaillou. Davis also focused on one village in telling the story of Martin Guerre's return to Artigat.[10] Ladurie's book showed that historians could use the accounts of, for example, an investigation by the Roman Catholic Church* into unconventional peasant religious beliefs in the thirteenth century. Such documents yielded a great deal of information about the prevailing customs, village social relations, the power of the Church, and popular beliefs about God, sexuality, death, marriage, magic, and time.[11] This was a powerful example of using hard evidence to explore how people lived and discover facts that may not have been obvious from regular archives.

In Italy, historian Carlo Ginzburg led the way to microhistory,* a new discipline that took specific examples and saw them as offering clues to bigger themes. Ginzburg, like Davis and Ladurie, focused on one place. In his book, *The Cheese and the Worms: The Cosmos of a Sixteenth-Century Miller*, Ginzburg examined the worldview of Menocchio,* a miller and cheese-maker from Montereale, Italy.

Ginzburg wrote that, rather than viewing the world through the eyes of the Church, it should be viewed from Menocchio's point of view. He uses the example that when cheese-makers made cheese, a solid mass was formed out of milk curd and worms appeared in it (most likely because of the inability to refrigerate food properly at that time). Menocchio called these worms "angels" because he saw God's work in their ability to turn the milk curd into cheese.[12]

The Contemporary Debate

Davis drew on the work of both Ladurie and Ginzburg to challenge the position of scientific historians. In *The Return of Martin Guerre*, she demonstrated that it was possible to write about a French peasant with a combination of new methods, in particular by using her own imagination to fill in the gaps in the archival records.

"Emmanuel Le Roy Ladurie and Carlo Ginzburg came to write their splendid microhistories—the 1975 *Montaillou* of the former, the 1976 *Cheese and Worms* of the latter—as an expansion of their prose," Davis said. "I came to microhistory (or what I called ethnography*) via film. In my historian's book, I tried to make the 'prodigious tale' of Martin Guerre understandable in terms of everything I could find about village life."[13]

Davis's debt to these authors also became clear from the focus and scope of her work. *The Return of Martin Guerre* relies on Ladurie, for example, for important contextual information from village and regional cultures.[14] Davis chose to examine a specific story, set in a specific place, while also developing stories from legal records.[15]

NOTES

1 Peter Novick, *That Noble Dream: The "Objectivity Question" and the American Historical Profession* (Cambridge: Cambridge University Press, 1988), 40.

2 Natalie Zemon Davis, *The Return of Martin Guerre* (Cambridge, MA: Harvard University Press, 1983), 3.

3 Novick, *That Noble Dream*, 415.

4 Stephan Thernstrom, *Poverty and Progress: Social Mobility in a Nineteenth-Century City* (Cambridge, MA: Harvard University Press, 1964), 1

5 Pierre and Huguette Chaunu, *Séville et l'Atlantique (1504–1560)* ("Seville and the Atlantic"), 12 vols (Paris: Hachette, 1955–9).

6 Ernst A. Breisach, *American Progressive History: An Experiment in Modernization* (Chicago: University of Chicago Press, 1993), 83.

7 Natalie Zemon Davis, *A Life of Learning* (New York: American Council of Learned Societies, 1997), 18; Emmanuel Le Roy Ladurie, *Les Paysans de Languedoc* ("The Peasants of Languedoc"), 2 vols (Paris: SEVPEN, 1966).

8 Ladurie, *Les Paysans*, i. i–xxiv.

9 Ladurie, *Les Paysans*, ii. 248–53.

10 Emmanuel Le Roy Ladurie, *Montaillou: Village Occitain de 1294 à 1324* ("Montaillou: Languedoc Village from 1294 until 1324") (Paris: Gallimard, 1975).

11 Ladurie, *Montaillou*, 17.

12 Carlo Ginzburg, *The Cheese and the Worms: The Cosmos of a Sixteenth-Century Miller* (Baltimore, MD: Johns Hopkins University Press), 39.

13 Davis, *Life of Learning*, 19.

14 Davis, *The Return of Martin Guerre*, 3 n. 5, 52 n. 2.

15 Davis, *The Return of Martin Guerre*, 3.

MODULE 4
THE AUTHOR'S CONTRIBUTION

KEY POINTS

- Davis argued that women shaped their own fortunes using their intellectual and emotional intelligence. By looking at social customs, religion and marriage, she saw the story of Martin Guerre as transcending class lines.

- *The Return of Martin Guerre* turned existing accounts on their head. It shows how individuals used their roles in society for their benefit.

- Davis's conclusions stand alone in the field because only writers and poets had previously told the story of Martin Guerre—not historians.

Author's Aims

In *The Return of Martin Guerre*, Natalie Zemon Davis retells the story of Martin Guerre in order to examine the cultural history* of sixteenth-century France. She explores how new methods and interdisciplinary concepts could help her write a history based only on limited evidence. Underlying these general goals is her hope of discovering the truth about Arnaud du Tilh's impersonation of Martin Guerre.

As Davis explained, "Taking on someone else's name and person with intention to defraud was thought a serious crime in sixteenth-century France." So the story was "told and re-told because it reminds us that astonishing things are possible."[1] On the one hand, this is a tale of hope and proof of individual ingenuity. But it is also a tale that keeps the historian and the reader guessing. In the end, Arnaud's downfall is

> ❝ It is a fitting tribute to a leading American social historian of early-modern* France that she has helped shape a French film version of, as well as a written monograph on, the celebrated sixteenth-century story of Martin Guerre. ❞
>
> A. Lloyd Moote, review of *The Return of Martin Guerre*, *American Historical Review*

tragic for him and perhaps also for Martin's wife, Bertrande.

Davis's innovation comes from a combination of archival research, imagination, and literary narrative. She highlights the role of women in peasant society and the private emotional experiences of peasants. These include Martin's experience of marriage and Bertrande's experience of maintaining her honor.[2] Davis's version of the Martin Guerre story is, therefore, partly her invention, "but held tightly in check by the voices of the past."[3] Notably, the book is dedicated to her husband, Chandler Davis,* and Davis relies on her own experience of marriage to tell the story of Martin Guerre.[4] As she herself said, "It's wanting to bring people to life again as a mother would want to bear children."[5]

Approach

As a historian, Davis reconstructed the complex mindset of past peoples so that a reader could relive their experiences. This is an established philosophical goal of history, promoted by Davis and other scholars, including the English historian R. G. Collingwood.*[6] Collingwood insisted that historians should make it possible for their readers to relive the past as they read a history book.[7]

Davis uses methods from various fields, especially anthropology,* to reconstruct the tale. "As Berkeley had been a favorable site for my anthropological interests of the 1970s, so Princeton was a favorable site for my cinematic and literary interests of the 1980s," she explained."[8]

She worked with Clifford Geertz,* a leading anthropologist at Princeton, and borrowed his concept of "thick description" of a society.[9] Geertz argued that to fully understand societies, anthropologists should recognize the "scripts" that shape and explain social rituals. Geertz uses the word "scripts" in the sense of the invisible, generic scripts that actors might follow in a scene, for example when they meet a new person, or attend a dinner. Geertz viewed culture as a way to see the larger meaning in seemingly obscure or eccentric behavior.[10] Without understanding the context, an outsider would not understand behavior, Geertz said. For that reason Davis saw her task as decoding past cultures."Anthropology offers suggestions," she said, and historians should use it to deepen their methods.[11]

Davis also favored using the ideas of literary scholars. Her experience with film was key to the importance she placed on narrative, or storytelling. *The Return of Martin Guerre* unfolds chronologically, with the academic analysis of cultural and social developments woven into the narrative. It reads like a novel in the style of *The Wife of Martin Guerre*, a 1943 work of fiction by Janet Lewis.* An American novelist and poet, Lewis was the only twentieth-century author to write in English about Martin Guerre before Davis's book was published in 1983.[12]

Davis wanted her book to appeal to a popular, non-academic audience[13] And her use of narrative in *The Return of Martin Guerre* brought a literary quality to history that had been discouraged in the field until then. Her storytelling technique is a departure from the analysis of large quantities of statistical data favored by previous historians. But one of Davis's colleagues at Princeton, Lawrence Stone,* argued that the data could only go so far in telling a story.[14] Davis also added another element to her account by using illustrations—including one of a peasant couple resembling Martin and Bertrande—to bring the story to life.[15]

Contribution In Context

Davis's work achieved two goals in the 1980s. First, *The Return of Martin Guerre* reinterprets the story, examining interactions between economic classes, as well as exploring social and gender history. Second, her analysis employs the tools of cultural historians to show how cultural history could be told. This was new: a way of writing about history that was free of other historians' past obsessions with science and objectivity.

Davis's version of the story produced new insights about women's role in society and religion. Her defense of the use of narrative and imagination challenged the prevailing theories of historians in the 1980s. As Davis's friend Le Roy Ladurie* observed, ultimately statistics could tell historians only so much before they had to investigate "invisible spiritual frontiers that were more constraining than any others."[16] In other words, for Ladurie as for Davis, popular beliefs of the time held the key to understanding past eras.

NOTES

1   Natalie Zemon Davis, *The Return of Martin Guerre* (Cambridge, MA: Harvard University Press, 1983), 63, 125.

2   Davis, *The Return of Martin Guerre*, 98, 27.

3   Davis, *The Return of Martin Guerre*, 5; Natalie Zemon Davis, "On the Lame," *American Historical Review* 93 (1988): 574, 575.

4   Natalie Zemon Davis, *A Life of Learning* (New York: American Council of Learned Societies, 1997), 18–19.

5   Rob Harding, "Interview with Natalie Zemon Davis," in *Visions of History,* ed. Henry Abelove et al. (Manchester: Manchester University Press, 1983), 113.

6   Davis, "On the Lame," 575.

7   R. G. Collingwood, *The Idea of History* (Oxford: Oxford University Press, 1946), §2 "The Historical Imagination," 2311970s, 49.

8   Davis, *Life of Learning*, 19.

9   Davis, *Life of Learning*, 19.

10 Clifford Geertz, "Thick Description: Toward an Interpretive Theory of Cultures," in *The Interpretation of Cultures* (New York: Perseus, 1973), 5–6, 9–10.

11 Harding, "Interview," 112.

12 Janet Lewis, *The Wife of Martin Guerre* (Athens, OH: Ohio University Press), 1943.

13 Davis, "On the Lame," 574–6.

14 Lawrence Stone, "The Revival of Narrative: Reflections on a New Old History," *Past and Present* 85 (1979): 3–24.

15 Davis, *The Return of Martin Guerre*, xiii, xiv, 45.

16 Emmanuel Le Roy Ladurie, *Les Paysans de Languedoc* ("The Peasants of Languedoc"), 2 vols (Paris: SEVPEN, 1966), i, 11.

SECTION 2
IDEAS

MAIN IDEAS

KEY POINTS

- Davis focuses on the role of women, identity, self-fashioning* — the process of constructing one's public persona according to socially acceptable norms — and interactions between people of different cultures and classes.

- One of Davis's main arguments is that historians must understand the social and cultural context of their research to draw accurate conclusions.

- The author presents her observations, views, and ideas with scholarly arguments and observations in a narrative that, although written by a historical scholar, reads like a detective story.

Key Themes

The Return of Martin Guerre presents a new version of the Guerre story using three key themes. First, Natalie Zemon Davis argues that Martin's wife Bertrande plays a vital role in helping Arnaud du Tilh impersonate Martin. To prove her theories, Davis uses extensive records and other research into peasant life in the sixteenth century.

Second, Bertrande, Arnaud, and the villagers of Artigat have considerable freedom to reinvent their identities. They do this by adopting new religious rituals and social customs, and by changing their personal appearance. Third, Davis describes cultural integration* — the ways in which people seek to join social groups by learning new customs, behavior, and language. This occurs when members of different social and economic classes interact.

Importantly, Davis argues that Bertrande is not a passive victim in

> 66 Historians have been learning more and more about rural families from marriage contracts and testaments, from parish records of births and deaths, and from accounts of courtship rituals and charivaris [wedding celebrations]. But we still know rather little about the peasants' hopes and feelings; the ways in which they experienced the relation between husband and wife, parent and child, the ways in which they experience the constraints and possibilities in their life. 99
>
> Natalie Zemon Davis, *The Return of Martin Guerre*

the fraudulent marriage, adding a new twist to the story. Instead, Davis writes, Bertrande assists Arnaud and does not view him as a criminal. Both Bertrande and Arnaud reinvent themselves as a married couple.

Arnaud is perhaps smarter than the judges in the criminal case brought against him—his intelligence is remarkable because of the judges' superior class status.[1] It was most unusual that an uneducated peasant could be cleverer than a judge.

Exploring The Ideas

Davis's interpretation of Bertrande's role in the fraudulent marriage helps her make the case that women played a greater role in society than previous studies of early-modern* Europe had suggested. At the age of 16, Bertrande already displays "a concern for her reputation as a woman, a stubborn independence, and a shrewd realism about how she can maneuver within the constraints placed upon her sex."[2]

Davis accepts that women are less powerful than men, at least in the public sphere. But she notes that Bertrande is shrewd, working "to calculate her advantages." There are significant advantages to be gained, too, because women hold important positions in the Artigat community. "A wife of Artigat ... could hope to enjoy the respect of other village women and informal power as a widow, being addressed by the worthy title of Na, able to bestow a vineyard on a newly married son and hosen on all her godchildren."[3] So within certain legal bounds women have a degree of control over their social status and power. Bertrande's role in village society also offers clues as to how she and Arnaud are able to convince the public that Martin Guerre himself is an imposter.

Several years after Martin's departure, Arnaud appears in Artigat claiming to be Martin Guerre. For the most part the villagers welcome him, as does Bertrande some time later.[4] Davis points out that Bertrande must have realized Arnaud was an imposter—she would, for example, have recognized that his "touch" while they were sexually intimate was not the same as Martin's. Bertrande and Arnaud are better lovers, Davis maintains, than Bertrande and Martin.[5]

Bertrande and Arnaud spend days and nights talking about ways to create their fictional marriage. "Among other things, so one must surmise, they decided to make the invented marriage last," Davis writes. Marriage was "something that was in their hands to make."[6]

After Arnaud is convicted, Bertrande works to clear his name. She pays to have his papers sent from the local court near Artigat to the appeals court in Toulouse, the capital city in southwestern France.

But then as a witness at Arnaud's trial, Bertrande "had to manipulate the image of the woman—easily-deceived, a skill that women often displayed before officers of justice any time it was to their advantage" in case Arnaud lost the appeal. Urged on by her Uncle Pierre, Bertrande acts as a passive witness in the male-dominated justice system so she can protect herself in the aftermath of this legal challenge to Arnaud's identity.[7]

Language And Expression

Throughout *The Return of Martin Guerre* Davis's language is appealing and direct. Non-academic readers can simply enjoy the fascinating story of Martin's disappearance and Arnaud's impersonation of him, and ignore the endnotes and chapters 10 and 11 that focus exclusively on sixteenth-century culture. Davis tells the tale chronologically, with the book resembling a "detective novel."[8] She intended it to read like a mystery so it would attract as wide an audience as possible.[9] For this reason *The Return of Martin Guerre* is Davis's best-known work of history with the general public. It has been translated into 22 languages and enjoyed a significant international circulation.[10]

Davis's use of plain language suits a story that began as an oral history and has been passed down by ordinary people through the generations. Residents of Artigat still talk about Martin Guerre today, Davis writes. She recalled that a recent immigrant from French Catalonia complained to her grandmother that "nothing ever happens in Artigat." "Perhaps not now," the grandmother replied. "But in the sixteenth century …" And she then related the story of Martin Guerre.[11]

NOTES

1   Natalie Zemon Davis, *The Return of Martin Guerre* (Cambridge, MA: Harvard University Press, 1983), ix.

2   Davis, *Return of Martin Guerre*, 28.

3   Davis, *Return of Martin Guerre*, 31.

4   Davis, *Return of Martin Guerre*, 42.

5   Davis, *Return of Martin Guerre*, 34.

6   Davis, *Return of Martin Guerre*, 46–7.

7   Davis, *Return of Martin Guerre*, 76.

8   Natalie Zemon Davis, "History's Two Bodies," *American Historical Review* 93 (1988).

9   Marnie Hughes-Warrington, "Natalie Zemon Davis," in *Fifty Key Thinkers on History* (London: Routledge, 2003), 59.

10 Barbara B. Diefendorf and Carla Hesse, *Culture and Identity in Early-Modern Europe 1500–1800: Essays in Honor of Natalie Zemon Davis* (Ann Arbor, MI: Michigan University Press, 1993), 262–5.

11 Davis, *Return of Martin Guerre*, 125.

MODULE 6
SECONDARY IDEAS

KEY POINTS

- *The Return of Martin Guerre* investigates the role of religion in peasant society, the implications of the law on concepts of justice, Basque* culture, family customs, and the role of individual behavior in creating identity.

- These secondary ideas form an important foundation for Davis in developing her main ideas.

- Davis's research on religion and law proved innovative.

Other Ideas

The Return of Martin Guerre relies on an array of secondary ideas that are important because they underpin Davis's new approach to the Martin Guerre story. There are four main secondary subjects. The first of these is popular sixteenth-century religious belief in France, particularly the arrival of Protestantism* following the Reformation.* Religion played no role in previous accounts of Martin Guerre's story, so Davis showed great insight by including it.[1]

Second is the importance of the rule of law,* both in mediating social interactions between the Guerre family (from the Basque region of France, on the border with Spain) and Arnaud du Tilh, a regular Frenchman. Third, family customs are a key part of the narrative, especially the Basque family customs in the Guerre family. Fourth, the book also examines the importance of behavior as a guide to a person's character, together with community and individual values like honor, courage, and loyalty.

> ❝I also want to explain why a story that seemed fit
> for a mere pamphlet—and indeed was told in that
> form—became in addition the subject for a judge's
> 'one hundred and eleven beautiful annotations'; and to
> suggest why we have here a rare identification between
> the fate of peasants and the fate of the rich and learned.❞
>
> Natalie Zemon Davis, *The Return of Martin Guerre*

Exploring The Ideas

Protestant beliefs emphasized the importance of faith as a personal matter in relation to an individual's conscience. Davis argues that the arrival of these ideas in regions near Artigat enabled Arnaud and Bertrande to believe they had the power to invent their marriage. Roman Catholic* doctrine, the most dominant religion at the time, held "that a wife was not free to remarry in the absence of her husband, no matter how many years elapsed, unless she had certain proof of his death."[2] Davis observes that "it is possible, even probable, that the new Martin and Bertrande de Rols were becoming interested in the new religion, in part because they could draw from it another justification of their lives."[3]

Davis argues that Protestantism permitted clandestine marriages. Protestant belief held variations on a theme that a woman could remarry after a year if her husband had deserted her, and that she need not necessarily remarry in public, nor be married by a priest with a licence. Although this did not conform to the law and custom of the Roman Catholic Church, it was legally valid, and was also valid according to Protestant canon law.

Effectively it became possible for Bertrande—whose family converted to Protestantism after Martin returned in 1560—to dare to think outside the bounds of traditional Catholicism.[4] Indeed, Jean de

Coras,* one of the judges in Arnaud's trial, had written a book about secret marriages among Protestants. He wrote it shortly before Arnaud's trial, so he may well have known about the fraudulent marriage.[5]

Davis's presentation of Arnaud's trials, meanwhile, emphasizes the way peasants used their legal rights to mediate conflicts in their family and social affairs. She does not represent Arnaud as a criminal, even though he is on trial for committing crimes. Davis's understanding of these legal interactions can be seen in an issue that arises between Arnaud and Pierre, Bertrande's uncle. Pretending to be Martin, and newly arrived in Artigat, Arnaud asks Pierre for records of his ancestral farmlands. As was traditional at the time, Pierre (acting as guardian for Martin's land) has put down a deposit on this land and is using it on the understanding that if and when Martin returns, he will return the land to its rightful owner [6] So there is a legal precedent that frames the way the two men deal with such a dispute.

The role of the villagers of Artigat at Arnaud's trial is important and the judges listen to the oral testimony of the peasants. Pierre attempts to admit evidence from a soldier passing through Artigat who told some villagers that Arnaud could not be Martin because the real Martin was alive in Spain.[7] Then, as now, the court regarded hearsay with caution and does not give it the same weight as testimony from a direct witness to the events in question.[8] The court also tries to admit inadmissible evidence by calling Arnaud's brothers to testify against him, which was forbidden by medieval law.[9] Arnaud himself nearly escapes conviction thanks to the old principle of Roman law "'that it was better to leave unpunished a guilty person than to condemn an innocent one.'"[10]

Davis also shows how regional customs shape migrant family identities. She explores the tension experienced by immigrants in holding onto old customs and accepting new ones in places where they settle, such as Artigat. The Guerre family has moved from the

Basque region of France, close to the Spanish border; Arnaud comes from Languedoc, an area of France that has different cultures and traditions. Part of Arnaud's undoing is the fact that he is not as familiar with Basque customs as Martin clearly would be. The Guerres have retained their Basque language and customs, while also integrating into the culture of Artigat.

This clash of cultures also has an impact on the previously-mentioned issue of farmland involving Bertrande's uncle, Pierre Guerre, who is himself Basque. It is Arnaud's intention to sell Martin Guerre's farmland, but in Basque society it was not permitted to sell inherited land. Arnaud's view is consistent with the emergence of capitalism* (the buying and selling of goods and services for profit) in the rural French economy of the sixteenth century.[11] However, Arnaud's ignorance of Basque culture creates doubts about his identity as the real Martin.[12]

Davis views the everyday behavior of people of all classes in the sixteenth century as important, because this was how different classes formed impressions of each other. The trial judge Jean Le Coras uses "manner as an index of good faith in the witnesses."[13] In other words, the judge considers that the way the witnesses—including peasants from a class far inferior to that of the judge—behave in court is the best guide to evaluating their reliability. Coras views Bertrande favorably because she has lived "'virtuously and honorably." He also says that her "uncertain and nervous manner during the confrontation" with Arnaud in court in May 1560 persuades him that Bertrande's uncle has forced her to bring her case against Arnaud.[14]

Overlooked

These secondary themes are important offshoots of the main ideas in *The Return of Martin Guerre*, but they are not necessarily part of what has created Davis's reputation as a scholar. She remains best known for her great contributions to cultural and gender history, not religious, legal, or family history.[15] This doesn't mean scholars completely overlook these secondary ideas, rather that they are part of the bigger themes Davis writes about. Ongoing examinations of *The Return of Martin Guerre* emphasize these broader cultural histories, with the result that Arnaud's trial "was used to reveal the expectations and possibilities a given village society made available to either sex."[16]

NOTES

1   Robert Finlay, "The Refashioning of Martin Guerre," *American Historical Review* 93 (1988): 555.

2   Natalie Zemon Davis, *The Return of Martin Guerre* (Cambridge, MA: Harvard University Press, 1983), 33.

3   Davis, *Return of Martin Guerre*, 48.

4   Davis, *Return of Martin Guerre*, 46, 49.

5   Jean de Coras, *Petit discours … Des Mariages Clandestinement et Irreverement Contractes* (1558).

6   Davis, *Return of Martin Guerre*, 53.

7   Davis, *Return of Martin Guerre*, 78.

8   Davis, *Return of Martin Guerre*, 78.

9   Davis, *Return of Martin Guerre*, 85.

10 Davis, *Return of Martin Guerre*, 81.

11 Davis, *Return of Martin Guerre*, 52.

12 Davis, *Return of Martin Guerre*, 51–4.

13 Davis, *Return of Martin Guerre*, 80.

14 Davis, *Return of Martin Guerre*, 80.

15 Judith P. Zinsser, "Women's History/Feminist History," in *The Sage Handbook of Historical Theory*, ed. Nancy Partner and Sarah Foot (London: Routledge, 2013), 256.

16 Olwen Hufton, "Women, Gender and the *Fin de Siècle*," in *Companion to Historiography*, ed. Michael Bentley (London: Routledge, 1999), 933.

MODULE 7
ACHIEVEMENT

KEY POINTS

- Natalie Zemon Davis believes her book allowed her to find out the truth about the story of Martin Guerre, as far as her sources permitted.

- Davis's accessible writing style and her work on a 1982 film version of the story of Martin Guerre—and a strong interest among historians in the cultural turn*—created a ready-made audience for the book.

- Davis's view of history as a conversation between historians and the past led some to wonder if her use of imagination to interpret facts goes too far.

Assessing The Argument

Natalie Zemon Davis herself admits there is insufficient evidence to justify some of her conclusions in *The Return of Martin Guerre*. But she believes her 1983 version of the story achieved her goals. According to her, imagining herself in another time and place, and using evidence and sources not directly related to the story to draw conclusions, does not conflict with her role as a historian. What is certain is that Davis achieved her goal of drawing attention to cultural and gender history in using her interdisciplinary method.

In the Introduction to the book, she writes, "My hope is to show that the adventures of three young villagers are not too many steps beyond the more common experience of their neighbors, that an imposter's fabrication has links with more ordinary ways of creating personal identity."[1] Davis cut to the core of human experience in the sixteenth century by the way she examined her material, and this has

> 66 It seems to me that we should be interested in the history of both women and men, that we should not be working only on the subjected sex any more than an historian of class can focus exclusively on peasants. Our goal is to understand the significance of the *sexes*, of gender groups in the historical past. Our goal is to discover the range in sex roles and in sexual symbolism in different societies and periods, to find out what meaning they had and how they functioned to maintain the social order or to promote its change. 99
>
> Natalie Zemon Davis, speaking at the Second Berkshire Conference on the History of Women, October 1975, quoted in Joan Kelly, *Women, History and Theory: The Essays of Joan Kelly*

fulfilled her primary purpose of telling the truth about that period of French history. It did so because it considered all sectors of society, from the peasant Guerre family right up to the noble judge, Jean le Coras.

Achievement In Context

The successful publication of *The Return of Martin Guerre* in 1983 was based to a large degree on the success of the 1982 French film, *Le Retour de Martin Guerre,** on which Davis had acted as a historical consultant. The film was very popular, the book further developed its themes, and so the two should be seen and read together.[2] As Davis put it, "the 1982 film *Le Retour de Martin Guerre* was a very good one, I thought." But she had realized early on, she said, that she "had to write an historian's book on the subject. Bertrande was being simplified for the screen in ways which deprived her of agency and her full dramatic complexity."[3]

Academic history required more than popular film-making could convey, and Davis insisted that the two approaches should go hand in hand: one was not capable of replacing the other. She believed in examining characters in detail. Her method was to use extensive research from the archives, along with a deep reading of literature about the sixteenth century. Davis felt that historians had a responsibility to use film to attract audiences to historical topics; in doing so they could then bring historical knowledge to a wider public. "The film review sections in historical journals and the existence of special periodicals on film and history are a real contribution," she said. "Historians might profitably contribute reviews in newspapers, on the radio, or on television. It's up to historians, those who have participated in the film and those who have seen it, to bring to the debate both an understanding of the possibilities of film and a knowledge of the past."[4]

Davis's cultural reading of the past, of the way she looked at the roles of ignored individuals and groups in shaping events, spread among historians. Scholars began to ask about the "historyless"[5]—a term from Howard Zinn's* widely read *A People's History of the United States,* published in 1980. Zinn's purpose was not to write history exclusively from the point of view of the victors of wars or the leading industrialists of the world. Instead, he saw a crucial need to tell the histories of ignored groups like slaves and workers, and the need to study discrimination against what he called the "racially and sexually dominated." Historians, he wrote, were "not to be on the side of executioners."[6] This movement was to become known as the cultural turn.

Academic interest in "historyless" people came about just as a revolution in American society, which started in the 1960s and 1970s, was taking hold. There was a growing tolerance and acceptance of individuals and social groups regardless of their class, race, gender, sexuality, or other unconventional traits. After the US Supreme Court* made abortion legal in 1973, women suddenly had the right to choose if they were going to have a baby. A variety of groups campaigned for equality between men and women at home and in the workplace. Others pushed for equal rights for homosexuals—an issue still relevant today as the debate over gay marriage continues in the United States.

All of these moves challenged established social norms—and the public was receptive to some of these developments. "Attitudes toward abortion were resistant to change; but on gay rights and feminism, public opinion polls in the 1980s and 1990s found a population growing less polarized despite the alarms and calls to battle, rather than more so."[7]

Limitations

As some historians see it, Davis's reliance on imaginative writing calls the credibility of *The Return of Martin Guerre* into question. Although she is careful to distinguish fact from fiction, fiction still creeps in. Throughout the book—on at least 32 of the 125 pages—the narrative is strewn with the words "perhaps" or "I think."[8] In her presentation of Bertrande, for example, Davis prefaces what she knows about the character by saying, "So far as we can see, Bertrande spent her childhood with at least one brother and close to her mother's side."[9] On other significant aspects of the story no hard evidence is offered. For example, Davis writes that "Bertrande had learned of that adult woman's world from her own mother, from her Basque* mother-in-law, and her godmother,"[10] but she has no proof that this is true.

Tensions between the film and book versions of *The Return of Martin Guerre* also led to criticism of the book by scholars fundamentally opposed to any alterations to historical narratives on screen. Because Davis had acted as a consultant on the Martin Guerre film, she was guilty by association (of potentially misrepresenting a chapter of French history) and to some degree this limited the impact of her book, at least with scholars.[11] By some it was seen as nothing more than a by-product of the film. Yet at least one reviewer supported the association between book and film, saying "Renaissance scholars— at least those who value historical imagination and have not lost their sense of wonderment—should find it illuminating as well as enjoyable. See the movie—but more especially read the book."[12]

NOTES

1   Natalie Zemon Davis, *The Return of Martin Guerre* (Cambridge, MA: Harvard University Press, 1983), 2.

2   Melissa E. Biggs, *French Films, 1945–1993* (Jefferson, NC: McFarland, 1993), 232.

3   Natalie Zemon Davis, *A Life of Learning* (New York: American Council of Learned Societies, 1997), 19.

4   Natalie Zemon Davis, "Movie or Monograph? A Historian/Filmmaker's Perspective," *Public Historian* 25 (2003): 48.

5   Sabyasachi Bhattacharya, "History from Below," *Social Scientist* 11 (1983): 3.

6   Howard Zinn, *A People's History of the United States of America* (New York: HarperCollins, 1980), 56.

7   Daniel T. Rodgers, *Age of Fracture* (Cambridge, MA: Harvard University Press, 2011), 172.

8   Davis, *Return of Martin Guerre*, 10, 12, 14, 15, 16, 19, 21, 24, 27, 32, 37, 38, 39, 43, 48, 52, 55, 56, 57, 67, 70, 75, 77, 83, 84, 91, 98, 102, 107, 118, 123, 125.

9   Davis, *Return of Martin Guerre*, 27.

10 Davis, *Return of Martin Guerre*, 29.

11 Biggs, *French Films*, 230.

12 Donald R. Kelley, "Review of *The Return of Martin Guerre*," *Renaissance Quarterly* 37 (1984): 254.

MODULE 8
PLACE IN THE AUTHOR'S WORK

KEY POINTS

- Throughout her life, Natalie Zemon Davis has focused on the cultural history* of Europe, often focusing on the role of women, historical theory, and, more recently, the history of everyday life.

- Davis's book was an early stylistic breakthrough from which much of her later work flowed.

- *The Return of Martin Guerre* is Davis's best-known work and made her internationally famous.

Positioning

Natalie Zemon Davis discovered Martin Guerre's story by chance, but her interpretation of it in *The Return of Martin Guerre* is considered her most experimental work. Just before Davis left Berkeley around 1978, one of her graduate students showed her what the sixteenth-century judge Jean de Coras* had written about the case of Arnaud du Tilh.[1] As Davis said, her work had focused on social rituals even before she read Coras. She had looked at peasant rituals, including wedding celebrations, mourning, and other forms of popular expression. Her attraction to the story of Martin Guerre, she said, "grew out of the practice of anthropological history. Most of my writing until then had explored issues or motifs—such as charivaris,* mourning ritual, proverbs—over a few centuries. Though archival material came mostly from Lyon [a city in central France where Davis found extensive records], texts and examples were drawn from over all France, sometimes from all over Western Europe."[2] The story of Martin Guerre gave Davis the opportunity to focus on a specific case, after

> **❝** Culture and identity have been subjects of central importance in Natalie Davis's work, from her earliest studies in the social and religious history of sixteenth century Lyon to her current research on the cross-cultural experiences and exchanges of Europeans who went abroad in increasing numbers during the sixteenth and seventeenth centuries. **❞**
>
> Barbara B. Diefendorf and Carla Hesse, "Introduction: Culture and Identity," *Culture and Identity in Early Modern Europe (1500–1800)*

studying more general popular rituals.

The Return of Martin Guerre nevertheless distills the main threads that have continued to run throughout Davis's work. She has studied cultural, social, and religious history, with an emphasis on gender history. She has also focused on popular belief and historical method. Her book *Fiction in the Archives* (1987) is one of several publications about film and history. Her belief is that historians can draw new conclusions, writing narratives without evidence from archives. As Davis has said herself since *The Return of Martin Guerre,* "I think I've acquired a sort of style, or at least a habitual way of perceiving situations and people, that is of always looking for questions about self-fashioning,* of fashioning one's inner and outer self, and even imposture."[3]

These themes appeared in essays Davis wrote in 1975, before *The Return of Martin Guerre,* collected in *Society and Culture in Early Modern France: Eight Essays.*[4] In that collection, an essay entitled "Women on Top" begins, "The female sex was thought the disorderly one *par excellence* in early-modern* Europe."[5] Davis here investigates how a male-dominated society saw female behavior as disruptive to the social order. *Society and Culture* looks at the way such a view of female behavior could change ideas about religion, behavior, and customs.[6]

Integration

Davis's next steps drew on her early interests. In the 1980s she worked extensively on the relationship between cultural history and method, looking at the problem posed by cultural history. How can historians recreate and write about past cultures, when the evidence required for a complete and accurate picture often does not exist? *Fiction in the Archives* (1987) explored the stories of individuals from all ranks of French sixteenth-century society who sought pardons for their crimes from the king. The work developed Davis's idea that it is possible to imagine what must have happened in a particular case by inference, based on other contemporary documentation. Such accounts offered a window into the workings of the French legal system, something for which Davis had already been praised in *The Return of Martin Guerre*. She also looked at the creativity and resourcefulness of ordinary people, including simple peasants, in shaping their hopes for the future.[7]

Davis then turned to a project that combined all these interests, but which put women at the forefront. In *Women on the Margins*, published in 1995, she again showed her sympathy for early-modern women. Davis explored the ways in which religion both limited and gave structure to women's sense of self, describing the book as "a project that wove together all the strands of my past interests—social, anthropological, ethnographic, and literary—and yet also cast me out on new seas and territories."[8] As in *The Return of Martin Guerre*, this book featured a study of the lives of individuals and how they perceived and understood religious and social boundaries. The work enabled Davis to "expand the single microhistory* into a decentered comparison of three European lives":[9] a German-Jewish* merchant, a French Catholic,* and a German Protestant.*

Davis's more recent works also feature themes from *The Return of Martin Guerre*, with an even greater emphasis on women and their roles in society. In examining the cultural history of under-represented people, she has again explored the relationship between fiction, film, and history. Her most recent book, *Trickster Travels: In Search of Leo Africanus, a Muslim Between Worlds*, published in 2006, expanded her historical works from France to the rest of the world.[10] Here she examines the life of another obscure figure from the sixteenth century, Johannes Leo Africanus,* a Muslim born in Spain whose travels took him across Europe. The book considers culture, religion, sexual habits, social customs, tolerance, and violence. Davis collected extensive information about Africanus and his views of the world, especially of Africa.[11] While reconstructing the career of this brilliant storyteller she argues for a better understanding of the Muslim world. The timing of the work was not coincidental, being published at a time of great tension in the relationship between the West and Islam in the wake of the 9/11* terrorist attacks on the United States in 2001 and the subsequent US invasions of Afghanistan and Iraq.

Significance

The Return of Martin Guerre remains Davis's best-known work, both among the general population and historians.[12] The book and the film helped build Davis's reputation as a leading historian[13] and her profile grew substantially from the 1980s onwards.

Now in her late 80s, Davis is a respected elder in the field of history.[14] Her radical political activities in the 1960s and 1970s profoundly informed her research interests and throughout her career she has explored the stories and power of often-ignored groups such as women, slaves, and non-Europeans, exposing inequalities in past societies. Importantly, however, she has shown how these people have been able to retain control both over their lives and their dignity.

The Return of Margin Guerre should not overshadow Davis's other achievements as a cultural historian, and her intellectual interests have continued to evolve with the changing agendas in the field of history. In the late 1990s, for example, there was an emphasis on comparative and global history,* and in the early 2000s Davis and other historians branched out from Europe to study other regions.[15] In *Trickster Travels* (2006), she examines the relationships between slaves and Jewish colonizers in eighteenth-century Surinam.* Yet, true to the approach she took with the story of Martin Guerre, this book again highlights unexpected and unusual historical relationships. It is another example of Davis "reading against the grain."[16]

NOTES

1   Natalie Zemon Davis, *A Life of Learning* (New York: American Council of Learned Societies, 1997), 17.

2   Davis, *Life of Learning*, 17.

3   Natalie Zemon Davis, *A Passion for History: Conversations with Denis Crouzet* (Kirksville, MO: Truman State University Press, 2010), 10.

4   Natalie Zemon Davis, *Society and Culture in Early Modern France: Eight Essays* (Stanford, CA: Stanford University Press, 1975).

5   Natalie Zemon Davis, *The Return of Martin Guerre* (Cambridge, MA: Harvard University Press, 1983), 124.

6   Davis, "Strikes and Salvation at Lyon," "The Rites of Violence," in *Society and Culture*, 1–16, 152.

7   Leigh Buchanan Bienen, "The Law as Storyteller: *The Return of Martin Guerre* by Natalie Zemon Davis," *Harvard Law Review* 98 (1984): 494–502; Natalie Zemon Davis, *Fiction in the Archives: Pardon Tales and their Tellers in Sixteenth-Century France* (Stanford, CA: Stanford University Press, 1987).

8   Davis, *Life of Learning*, 21.

9   Davis, *Life of Learning*, 21.

10 Natalie Zemon Davis, *Trickster Travels: In Search of Leo Africanus, A Muslim Between Worlds* (London: Faber, 2006).

11 Davis, *Trickster Travels*, 31–47.

12 Marnie Hughes-Warrington, "Natalie Zemon Davis," in *Fifty Key Thinkers on History* (London: Routledge, 2003), 59.

13 Natalie Zemon Davis, "On the Lame," *American Historical Review* 93 (1988): 573.

14 Jean-Christophe Agnew, "Capitalism, Culture and Catastrophe," in *The Cultural Turn in US History: Past, Present & Future*, ed. James W. Cook and Lawrence B. Glickman (Chicago: University of Chicago Press, 2008), 391.

15 See Ulinka Rublack, ed., *A Concise Companion to History* (Oxford: Oxford University Press, 2011), 65.

16 Natalie Zemon Davies, "David Nassy's Furlough and the Slave Mattheas," in *New Essays in American Jewish History Commemorating the Sixtieth Anniversary of the Founding of the Jewish Archives*, ed. Pamela Nadell (Cincinatti, OH: American Jewish Archives, 2012): 79–94.

SECTION 3
IMPACT

MODULE 9
THE FIRST RESPONSES

KEY POINTS

- Robert Finlay,* an American historian of sixteenth-century Italy, put forward the most serious critique of Natalie Zemon Davis's work. He argued that Davis's evidence simply did not prove her conclusions.

- Davis's response offered a strong defense of detective work and reimagining history, using techniques from subjects like anthropology.*

- The overwhelming response to *The Return of Martin Guerre* was positive, driven by the high demand for cultural histories at the end of the twentieth century.

Criticism

American historian Robert Finlay wrote the sharpest criticism of Natalie Zemon Davis's *The Return of Martin Guerre* in the *American Historical Review*, the official publication of the American Historical Association.*[1] Finlay's perspective was very different from that of Davis.[2] He worked on early-modern* European history, studying popular political ideas in Venice, Italy, and drew his conclusions based on the written work of diarists and chroniclers such as the sixteenth-century Croatian scholar Andronicus Tranquillus Parthenius.* Finlay focused on politics, rather than culture or society, and he had plenty of archival resources available to him compared to records on peasant life.

Finlay's main criticism of *The Return of Martin Guerre* was that it was a work of fiction rather than a work of history. He stated that, "Whatever the accuracy of Davis's view of peasant society, her application of that perspective to the story of Martin Guerre does not

> ❝ In sum, Davis presents a scenario in which the principal participants in a trial—the plaintiff, the defendant, and the judges—harbored secret designs and motivations that, by their very nature, cannot be substantiated by the sources. ❞
>
> Robert Finlay, "Refashioning Martin Guerre"

yield a portrait of Bertrande that is either plausible or persuasive."[3]

Finlay rejected Davis's argument that Bertrande *must* have known that Arnaud was not Martin because Bertrande enjoyed better sexual relations with Arnaud than she had with Martin. Finlay argued that Bertrande and Martin had so little sexual experience that Bertrande could not have recognized Arnaud as an impostor based on that evidence.[4] He also claimed that Davis had failed to explain why Bertrande did not remove her name as a witness against Arnaud for stealing Martin's identity, which would have been the "safest" course of action for Bertande and Arnaud. He insisted that even if her uncle, Pierre Guerre, had pressured her to sign, the collapse of the case would bring Arnaud home and restore Bertrande's honour and marital protection.[5]

Finlay had two specific problems with Davis's theories in the book. One, that she had insufficient evidence to support her argument that the arrival of Protestantism* and its alternative approach to issues of marriage—particularly remarriage if a wife is deserted by her husband—did in fact allow for clandestine marriages in a way that the Catholic Church did not. And two, the notion that the trial judge, Jean de Coras, and the accused, Arnaud du Tilh, had great respect for each other.[6]

Finlay also suspected that the characters in *The Return of Martin Guerre* were "more compelling for a modern sensibility" because Davis viewed them through the lens of modern fields like psychology.[7] Davis, he argued, projected theories held by current psychologists onto the main characters—Arnaud, Bertrande, and Martin—and he concluded that they would not have recognized Davis's descriptions of them. In Finlay's view, Davis was not using serious anthropology* and was ultimately injecting the present into the past.

Responses

Finlay's criticisms of *The Return of Martin Guerre* together with Davis's response to them were published in a single 1988 edition of the *American Historical Review*, in what was called "The Martin Guerre Forum."

In defending her version of events, Davis took issue with Finlay, saying his view was morally simplistic and rigid. "The rights and wrongs in the Guerre case are also crystal clear to Finlay, and he attributes similar moralism—a wrongful and romantic moralism—to me," Davis wrote.[8] Finlay argued, however, that no one could even prove Bertrande had helped Arnaud at all, let alone helped him fabricate their false marriage.

Davis supports her position by invoking sixteenth-century philosophy that emphasized the difficulty of learning the truth of a matter. Her response to Finlay uses the title of an essay by French philosopher Michel de Montaigne,* "On the Lame," which is also the name of a chapter in *The Return of Martin Guerre*.[9] In his essay, Montaigne discusses how difficult it is to get to the truth and how uncertain even the most seemingly logical conclusions can be. So Davis's response to Finlay leaves open the idea that she may indeed have reached the wrong conclusions. The records on which Davis based her book stated that Martin Guerre returned to Bertrande at the end of Arnaud du Tilh's trial. But at the end of the article Davis acknowledges records that show a Martin Guerre being executed in Spain for spying in 1555. However, it is still unclear whether the records of Martin Guerre's execution refer to the same Martin Guerre as in the story.[10]

Davis's response also repeats the central arguments of *The Return of Martin Guerre* to show that she had not altered her position as a result of Finlay's critique. Once more she outlined the sources she used for the book, and then explained why she wrote the account of Bertrande in the way she did: "First, let me spell out for readers my research method," she begins after a lengthy introduction. "We will begin with Bertrande de Rols and what she 'knew' about Arnaud du Tilh when they lived together as husband and wife."[11]

Davis remained firm in spite of Finlay's skepticism. "I establish beyond the shadow of a doubt," she explained, "the presence of converts, pastors, and religious action in the region around Artigat in the late 1550s, a good decade before the inhabitants of Artigat cleansed the church and were described in local manuscripts as Huguenots."* Huguenots were members of the French Protestant Church.[12]

Conflict And Consensus

Davis did not change her account of Martin Guerre's story after the debate with Finlay. There was agreement that *The Return of Martin Guerre* made a valuable contribution to the study of sixteenth-century French history. The book made both Arnaud du Tilh and the town where the story takes place—Artigat—an important example of how to focus on individual, local, and regional history. Scholars of the sixteenth century remarked that "Arnaud du Tilh has joined Domenico de Scandella (Menocchio* in Carlo Ginzburg's *The Cheese and the Worms*) as a famous 'common man' of the 1500s."[13] Despite Finlay's negative opinion, there was general consensus that Davis had done the most thorough research that could be expected of a historian, given the state of the relevant archives.[14]

The story of Martin Guerre has remained "one of the most famous and frequently recounted" stories of French history of the sixteenth century, according to David Potter,* a British scholar and expert on early-modern France. He felt Davis had raised questions about the motives of Bertrande, her family, and the Artigat villagers, but that we still do not have complete answers: "To none of these questions are definitive answers really possible, though Dr. Davis has probably done as much as anyone could to understand them."[15] This is true, but Davis has nonetheless managed to flesh out "an historical psychology of the sixteenth century"[16] by studying the emotional and intellectual lives of ordinary French people.

NOTES

1   Robert Finlay, "The Refashioning of Martin Guerre," *American Historical Review* 93 (1988); Natalie Zemon Davis, "On the Lame," *American Historical Review* 93 (1988).

2   Robert Finlay, *Politics in Renaissance Venice* (London: Ernest Benn, 1980), iii–ix.

3   Finlay, "Refashioning," 557.

4   Finlay, "Refashioning," 558–9.

5   Finlay, "Refashioning," 561.

6   Finlay, "Refashioning," 563.

7   Finlay, "Refashioning," 566.

8   Davis, "On the Lame," 598.

9   Natalie Zemon Davis, *The Return of Martin Guerre* (Cambridge, MA: Harvard University Press, 1983), 114–22; Davis, "On the Lame," 597.

10 Davis, "On the Lame," 603.

11 Davis, "On the Lame," 574–5, 576–84.

12 Davis, "On the Lame," 590.

13 William Monter, "Review of the *The Return of Martin Guerre*," *Sixteenth Century Journal* 14 (1983): 516.

14 Donald R. Kelley, "Review of *The Return of Martin Guerre*," *Renaissance Quarterly* 37 (1984): 252; Robert J. Knecht, "Review of *The Return of Martin Guerre*," *History* 70 (1985): 121; Emmanuel Le Roy Ladurie, "Review of *The Return of Martin Guerre*," *New York Review of Books*, December 30, 1983; A Lloyd Moote, "Review of *The Return of Martin Guerre*," *American Historical Review* 90 (1985): 943.

15 David Potter, "Review of *The Return of Martin Guerre*," *English Historical Review* 101 (1986): 713, 714.

16 Daniel Fabre, "Review of *The Return of Martin Guerre*," *Annales. Histoire, Sciences Sociales* 41 (1986): 711.

MODULE 10
THE EVOLVING DEBATE

KEY POINTS

- *The Return of Martin Guerre* fueled interest in the role of gender, culture, popular beliefs, and social relationships.

- Davis's work may have depended on literary techniques, but she never claimed this was sufficient or that science-based history was of no value.

- Many of Davis's own students have continued her work, developing their own approaches out of her framework.

Uses And Problems

In 1976, Nathalie Zemon Davis said, "study of the sexes should help promote a rethinking of some of the central issues faced by historians—power, social structure, property, symbols, and periodization."[1] Indeed, she had always been an outspoken supporter of women's studies and, later, "gender studies" that included men. Much earlier in her career, in the late 1960s, Davis helped design a course in women's history at the University of Toronto. This course included ideas relevant to the original story of *The Return of Martin Guerre*.[2] Gender was a "category or subject through which power acted."[3] This field of study "surged after 1990,"[4] as scholars looked at the role of male and female sexuality, as well as that of female power.

Leading French historians also followed in Davis's footsteps. They were scholars of what became known as the "new cultural history," an offshoot that developed out of Davis's own well-known work on cultural history.* The new focus challenged some of the fundamental ideas of Marxism* that Davis still believed in. "This new history maintained a paradoxical relationship to Marxism. It shared the

> ❝ By the later years of her career, [Natalie Zemon Davis's] influence had come to be felt far beyond the confines of American Reformation* scholarship. As of 1993, books of hers had been translated into nine languages. One of the most successful recent American manifestos for a 'new' history, Lynn Hunt's 1989 *New Cultural History*, invoked her as a patron saint. ❞
>
> Philip Benedict, "Between Whig Traditions and New Histories: American Historical Writing About the Reformation and Early Modern Europe"

Marxist view regarding the emancipatory function of historiography; but it understood the constraints from which men and women were to be emancipated quite differently."[5]

According to this new school of thought, constraints on individual power came not from politicians and power structures, but from interpersonal relationships between people. It was in those relationships that information could be found about discrimination, for example the existence of prejudiced ideas about both women and men based on gender and sexuality.[6]

Lynn Hunt,* an American scholar of French and global history, was outspoken about the tension between world history, now understood as global history, and the problem of writing the history of European everyday lives that ignores the everyday lives of those around the world. She explained that Dipesh Chakrabarty,* a historian from Bengal, "drew attention to the fact that Third World historians must read the leading works of European history, while European historians can ignore work from and about elsewhere because European historians provide a supposedly universal model for history scholarship."[7] Chakrabarty was critical of Davis, among others, for not embracing this more global view of history.

Schools Of Thought

The cultural history embodied by *The Return of Martin Guerre* straddles several schools of thought including women's history and feminism. Nevertheless, Davis carved out a unique niche that did not strictly follow any one school. Her conception of gender history in the 1960s showed a continuity with the efforts of scholars earlier in the twentieth century and before. This was clear to anyone looking at the bibliography Davis compiled for her 1960s women's history course at the University of Toronto. Bonnie G. Smith,* a specialist in gender history, wrote, "Thus the claim that women of the 1970s 'invented' women's history simply does not stand up to the evidence, which is not to discount that students and professors in the late 1960s and 1970s demanded courses in women's history, founded journals and held conferences."[8] Academics inspired by Davis's work pursued women's history, feminism, and cultural history, although with their own twists and agendas. None bought into Davis's approach completely, developing their own approaches to the problems they tackled.[9]

In terms of method, Davis's work also draws from various schools of thought and fields, including film studies. Some scholars argue that the boundary between history and fiction does not exist and that literary methods are key to understanding cultural history. They see multimedia and film as a way of enhancing our historical understanding. Yet in the academic battle against data-driven, "scientific history," Davis has never said that literary techniques alone were enough.[10] Her strong belief in the use of literary imagination brings her work close to that of historical theorists like Hayden White,* who identifies history itself as a form of fiction, or Frank Ankersmit,* who sees history as rhetoric—language that is specifically intended to influence people and that may not be entirely honest.[11] White considered that all historical work relied entirely on fictional devices: "(1) chronicle; (2) story; (3) mode of emplotment; (4) mode of argument; and (5) mode of ideological implication."[12]

Davis believes in the power of film to help historians reach a wider audience but she is wary of supporting it as a tool to help historians represent the past.[13] She said that "Cinema has a long way to go before its visual and dramatic conventions begin to catch up with the rules of evidence and the ways they are stated in historical prose."[14]

In Current Scholarship

Followers of Davis's methods and specialties in cultural history honored her by compiling a 1993 collection of essays, *Culture and Identity in Early Modern Europe.* The collection was published three years before she retired from the faculty at Princeton. Among Davis's former students who contributed to the collection were Carla Hesse,* Peter Sahlins,* and Barbara B. Diefendorf.*[15] They have all continued to follow Davis's style in their own accounts, using extensive research, evidence, and the latest concepts from the humanities and social sciences. Like their teacher, they have also injected an imaginative element into their work.

Carla Hesse combines Davis's interest in cultural theory and the role of gender and class mobility in early-modern* and modern French society.[16] She has also contributed to legal history, considering subjects such as the emergence of intellectual property laws during the French Revolution. Those laws dealt with copyright, or ownership of ideas; trademarks for retailers; and patents for inventers of technology.[17] In her writing, Hesse has shown how women were able to carve out new positions for themselves in French society, even when they were victims of discrimination.

Hesse and Peter Sahlins have worked together looking at the way people in early-modern France overcame class boundaries.[18] Sahlin's own work has focused on the relationship between peasants and the lower classes, and the formation of French national identity.[19] Barbara Diefendorf, meanwhile, has focused on French religious history.[20]

NOTES

1 Natalie Zemon Davis, "'Women's History' in Transition: The European Case," *Feminist Studies* 3 (1976): 90.

2 Bonnie G. Smith, "Gender I: From Women's History to Gender History," in *The Sage Handbook of Historical Theory*, ed. Nancy Partner and Sarah Foot (London: Routledge, 2013), 271.

3 Joan Scott quoted in Bonnie G. Smith, "Gender I: From Women's History to Gender History," in *The Sage Handbook of Historical Theory*, ed. Nancy Partner and Sarah Foot (London: Routledge, 2013), 273.

4 Smith, "Gender I," 274.

5 Georg G. Iggers, *Historiography in the Twentieth Century: From Scientific Objectivity to the Postmodern Challenge* (Middletown, CT: Wesleyan University Press, 1999), 99.

6 Iggers, *Historiography*, 99.

7 Lynn Hunt, *Writing History in a Global Era* (Boston: W. W. Norton and Company, 2014), 32.

8 Smith, "Gender I," 270.

9 Smith, "Gender I," 275.

10 Arthur M. Schlesinger, Jr., *A Life in the Twentieth Century: Innocent Beginnings, 1917–1950* (New York: Mariner, 2002), 44–7.

11 Hayden White, *Metahistory: The Historical Imagination of Nineteenth-Century Europe* (Baltimore, MD: Johns Hopkins University Press, 1973); Frank Ankersmit, *The Reality Effect in the Writing of History: The Dynamics of Historiographical Topology* (Amsterdam: Noord-Hollandsche, 1989).

12 White, *Metahistory*, 5.

13 Natalie Zemon Davis, *Slaves on Screen: Film and Historical Vision* (Cambridge, MA: Harvard University Press, 2002).

14 Monica Azzolini and Martyn Lyons, "Natalie Zemon Davis: An E-Mail Interview with Martyn Lyons and Monica Azzolini," *History Australia* 2 (2005): 91.3.

15 Barbara B. Diefendorf and Carla Hesse, *Culture and Identity in Early-Modern Europe 1500–1800: Essays in Honor of Natalie Zemon Davis* (Ann Arbor: Michigan University Press, 1993).

16 Carla Hesse, *The Other Enlightenment: How French Women Became Modern* (Princeton, NJ: Princeton University Press, 2001).

17 Carla Hesse, "The Rise of Intellectual Property, 700 B.C.–A.D. 2000: An Idea in the Balance," *Daedalus* 131 (2002): 6–45.

18 Carla Hesse and Peter Sahlins, "Mobility in France," special issue of *French Historical Studies* 29 (2006).

19 Peter Sahlins, *Unnaturally French: Foreign Citizens in the Old Regime and After* (Ithaca, NY: Cornell University Press, 2004).

20 Barbara B. Diefendorf, *The Saint Bartholomew's Day Massacre: A Brief History with Documents* (Boston: St. Martin's, 2008).

IMPACT AND INFLUENCE TODAY

KEY POINTS

- *The Return of Martin Guerre* remains both a popular and scholarly classic, which is a rare feat for a historian.

- The text continues to challenge those questioning the role of imagination and fiction in historical research, together with those who want to write histories of the lower classes around the globe.

- Scholars of a field known as subaltern studies* continue to challenge Davis's position and those of other cultural historians.

Position

Natalie Zemon Davis's *The Return of Martin Guerre* remains the key text in the telling of the story of Martin Guerre. It is also an important work for anyone who wants to learn about researching and writing cultural history.* Few historians have been as successful as Davis in advising film writers about how to represent a story for movie audiences.[1] The broad lens she applied to her study of Martin Guerre, meanwhile, helped the book remain important to scholars in many fields. Because Davis looks at a wide variety of issues, the text relies on several fields of study, including gender, cultural symbols, social customs, self-fashioning,* inter-class relations, and religion. Among the disciplines touched on are history, sociology, gender studies, historical theory, and other social sciences, with an emphasis on new perspectives that came from Davis's own political views. Her innovative methods, which she used to unearth new theories about the Martin Guerre story, inspire many historians today.[2] "Things don't have to be

> **❝**Named a Companion of the Order* for her contribution to social history, in particular, her focus on everyday people, [Natalie Zemon Davis] says that all success stories have 'a whole network' behind them, 'and you only get greatness in a country if you tend to, and care about, these others, who might not surface in the newspaper **❞**
>
> Erin Anderssen, "The Order of Canada: An Accolade that Demonstrates Why Waving the Flag Isn't Enough"

the way they are now," she once said in an interview. [3]

Interaction

Scholars have followed the threads in *The Return of Martin Guerre* on lots of different levels and in many different ways. In the afterword to a published interview several years ago, Davis wrote, "As I turn eighty-one, there is less urgency to my calling. I look around me and see generations of scholars doing every kind of history I ever hoped for, reformulating older questions and asking new ones."[4]

Two particular examples illustrate how scholars have examined and developed cultural history, drawing on *The Return of Martin Guerre*. First, Richard Burt,* a scholar of English literature, has expanded Davis's interests in the connection between storytelling, film, and literature. Among his projects, he has examined the role of modern mediums, including film, in bringing stories alive for readers and viewers.[5]

Second, Dorothy Ko,* a historian of China, continues to serve as an example of someone studying gender history and the role of women, as Davis did. Ko and her colleagues have produced key texts about Chinese feminism. The writings examine the rise of women's voices against inequality and discrimination in the country.[6] Because she focuses on China, Ko's work is more evidence of cultural history's reach across the globe.[7]

The Continuing Debate

Despite Davis's wide influence, new developments in history have still challenged her methods. For example, there is tension between cultural history's aim of giving voice to the voiceless—or the "historyless," as American historian Howard Zinn* described it—and new findings in global history.

Subaltern studies is a humanities discipline that focuses on the lives of people from colonized* countries in Southeast Asia. One goal for subaltern scholars is to end what they consider to be a European domination of historical accounts and instead to tell the stories of past peoples from the Third World.*[8] Global historians, meanwhile, want to abandon the twentieth-century fascination with European history.

Global history seeks to make history more relevant in the contemporary world. This often means comparing and contrasting religious practices in diverse parts of the world, rather than in just one country. The idea is to highlight the contributions and interactions of peoples worldwide.[9] French historians who came after Davis have branched out into global history. For the historian, this means thinking about "the local, the national, and the global, as well as the effects of their mutual reflexivity."[10] That is to say, historians should draw their conclusions while bearing in mind the local, national, and global aspects of what they are studying. In that sense, global history goes hand in hand with changing geopolitical relations. This can clearly be seen in, for example, the economic competition America and Europe now face from China, Russia, India, and Brazil.

Davis is aware of this new "global consciousness" and has contributed to the debate about the relationship between global and cultural history.[11] But her most recent book, *Trickster Travels*, published in 2006, tells the story of an upper-class diplomat and scholar, and consequently would not be well accepted by subaltern historians.

In 2011, Davis wrote that "the direct exchange among scholars across boundaries is one of the best paths to discovery of our globalized latter-day times."[12] In other words, examining the lives of scholars themselves demonstrates how the modern, globalized world has emerged. But would Davis's use of her own experience as a married woman in telling the French Martin Guerre story be as helpful in examining other cultures? For example, would that perspective be adequate for a historical account of a married Bengali woman from the sixteenth century, given the "uneven development of the past"[13] across the world?

Davis has actually prefaced conference papers about her latest work on individuals who moved across the world as "my own strategy to continue doing something local and concrete even though we're supposed to be doing something global and world history."[14]

NOTES

1   Melissa E. Biggs, *French Films, 1945–1993* (Jefferson, NC: McFarland, 1993), 238.

2   Bonnie G. Smith, "Gender I: From Women's History to Gender History," in *The Sage Handbook of Historical Theory*, ed. Nancy Partner and Sarah Foot (London: Routledge, 2013), 269.

3   Davis quoted in Peter Novick, *That Noble Dream: The "Objectivity Question" and the American Historical Profession* (Cambridge: Cambridge University Press, 1988), 462.

4   Natalie Zemon Davis, *A Passion for History: Conversations with Denis Crouzet* (Kirksville, MO: Truman State University Press, 2010), 183.

5   Richard Burt, *Medieval and Early Modern Film and Media* (Basingstoke: Palgrave Macmillan, 2008), 124–36.

6   Lydia H. Liu, Rebecca E. Karl, and Dorothy Ko, eds, *The Birth of Chinese Feminism: Essential Texts in Transnational Theory* (New York: Columbia University Press, 2013), 32.

7   Ko et al, *Chinese Feminism*.

8   Dipesh Chakrabarty, *Provincializing Europe: Postcolonial Thought and Historical Difference* (Princeton, NJ: Princeton University Press, 2000), 6–11, 74, 89.

9   Jerry H. Bentley, *Old World Encounters: Cross-Cultural Contacts and Exchanges in Pre-Modern Times* (Oxford: Oxford University Press, 1993), 115–43.

10 Herman Lebovics, *Bringing the Empire Back Home: France in a Global Age* (Durham, NC: Duke University Press, 2004), xvi.

11 Natalie Zemon Davis, "What is Universal About History?" in *Transnationale Geschichte: Themen, Tendenzen und Theorien*, ed. Gunilla Budde, Sebastian Conrad, and Oliver Janz (Göttingen: Vandenhoeck & Ruprecht, 2011), 18.

12 Natalie Zemon Davis, "Decentering History: Local Stories and Global Crossings in a Global World," *History and Theory* 50 (2011): 202.

13 Chakrabarty, *Provincializing Europe*, 239, 243.

14 Natalie Zemon Davis, "Decentering History," Holberg Prize Symposium 2010, accessed April 23, 2015, https://www.youtube.com/watch?v=IgacRhulA2E.

MODULE 12
WHERE NEXT?

KEY POINTS

- *The Return of Martin Guerre* will continue to stimulate research in cultural history* because it asks questions about understudied groups around the world that are still in many ways unanswered.

- Its impact comes, in part, from the inspiration it gave to Davis's students (and in turn their students) as well as to other researchers either with political agendas or unconventional views.

- It is an important work because of the fascinating story it revives, its radical cultural interpretation of that story, and the impact it had on historical research methods.

Potential

Natalie Zemon Davis's work in *Women on the Margins*, *Trickster Travels*, and *The Return of Martin Guerre* serves as a reminder of the power of stories from the past to connect with audiences and promote historical awareness. These books will be remembered as classic works of history, both because of their fascinating detail and the accessibility of their content thanks to Davis's writing.

The Return of Martin Guerre continues to speak to all historians who are investigating the scope of women's power in the early-modern* period. Susan Broomhall,* for example, who specializes in women's history and the history of emotions, has followed Davis's lead by exploring the religious and emotional lives of women in sixteenth-century France.[1]

The power of cultural history to bring personal stories to life

> **❝** My portrait is of a man with a double vision,
> sustaining two cultural worlds, sometimes imagining
> two audiences, and using techniques taken from the
> Arabic and Islamic repertoire while folding in European
> elements in his own fashion. **❞**
>
> Natalie Zemon Davis, *Trickster Travels: In Search of Leo Africanus,*
> *A Sixteenth-Century Muslim Between Worlds*

continues to attract graduate students and researchers. "The new
generation of scholars who are now entering the profession are
turning in new directions, to be sure, but they are not rejecting the
questions and preoccupations of those who trained them."[2] Some
cultural historians in America are now students of Davis's own
students, so her influence in the field of history is still apparent.[3]

Future Directions

Davis remains an important and well-known historian—a figurehead
for other historians. In 2012, she received the National Humanities
Medal in the United States in recognition of her considerable services
to history and to intellectual debate in North America.[4] She was also
named as a Companion of the Order of Canada* that same year,
because of her academic contributions at the University of Toronto
and her commitment to public causes aimed at improving the lives
of Canadians.[5]

Davis's work will likely stimulate historians eager to use history in
public service, so that they may learn from the stories she reports. They
can also draw from her ideas and her research to contribute to public
campaigns for equality and tolerance. She views history as a truly
human subject, which provides both scholars and readers with
understanding and hope. "No matter how bleak and constrained the
situation, some forms of improvisation and coping take place," Davis

wrote. "No matter what happens, people go on telling stories about it and bequeath them to the future. No matter how static and despairing the present looks, the past reminds us that change can occur. At least things can be different."[6]

Summary

The Return of Martin Guerre should first be read because it is a fascinating tale that leads readers to ask themselves who they are and how they relate to other people. This single case study provides a masterful insight into how individuals were shaped by wider social and cultural forces. Martin's abandonment of his wife and child, which happens immediately after the somewhat trivial incident of stealing grain from his uncle; Bertrande's struggle in a community which expects her to act as a faithful wife and mother in her husband's absence; and Arnaud's reinvention of himself, all present issues of truth and meaning that are relevant to everyone.

Davis's presentation of the story raises compelling issues about the practice of history itself. What is the nature of evidence? How can historians know if what they write is true? How can they use the concepts and findings of contemporary anthropology,* ethnography,* and social sciences to help them understand the past? Is it possible to explain a period of history using modern ideas that were not familiar to the people in the historical account? What, if anything, distinguishes history from fiction and film?

Finally, *The Return of Martin Guerre,* which reflects the peak of the era known as the cultural turn,* also pushes readers to think about the purpose of cultural history. It demonstrates the ingenuity of ordinary men—and, in particular, women—in sixteenth-century France. So cultural history is a way of restoring dignity to individuals in communities that have been long overlooked. These individuals deserve the respect and interest of modern readers and stand as case studies for survival in difficult times.

The Return of Martin Guerre also acts as a firm reminder of the power of history. As Davis herself said, "History offers us ideas, points of view, perspectives, landmarks, indices—possibilities."[7]

NOTES

1   Susan Broomhall, *Women and Religion in Sixteenth-Century France* (Basingstoke: Palgrave Macmillan, 2005).

2   Nathan Perl-Rosenthal, "Comment: Generational Turns," *American Historical Review* 117 (2012): 813.

3   Barbara B. Diefendorf and Carla Hesse, *Culture and Identity in Early-Modern Europe 1500–1800: Essays in Honor of Natalie Zemon Davis* (Ann Arbor: Michigan University Press, 1993), 7.

4   Christine Elias, "Natalie Zemon Davis Receives National Humanities Medal: Renowned Adjunct Professor of History Honoured," *University of Toronto News*, accessed April 23, 2015, http://news.utoronto.ca/natalie-zemon-davis-receives-national-humanities-medal.

5   Erin Anderssen, "The Order of Canada: An Accolade that Demonstrates Why Waving the Flag Isn't Enough," *The Globe and Mail,* June 30, 2012, accessed April 23, 2015, http://www.theglobeandmail.com/news/national/the-order-of-canada-an-accolade-that-demonstrates-why-waving-the-flag-just-isnt-enough/article4382059/?page=all.

6   Natalie Zemon Davis, *A Life of Learning* (New York: American Council of Learned Societies, 1997), 23.

7   Natalie Zemon Davis, *A Passion for History: Conversations with Denis Crouzet* (Kirksville, MO: Truman State University Press, 2010), 67.

GLOSSARY

GLOSSARY OF TERMS

American Historical Association: a professional body founded in 1884 of which many historians in America are members. Its role is to promote history and to lobby government on historical education, the preservation of records and manuscripts with historical value in the US, and access to those records for the public at large.

Annales **school:** a group of French historians and social scientists gathering around the journal the *Annales d'Histoire Economique et Sociale* ("Annals of Economic and Social History"), that was founded by Marc Bloch★ and Lucien Febvre★ in 1929. They shared ambitious methodological goals, such as comparative history and interdisciplinarity, and applied historical method to new objects of analysis such as climate and population trends, previously the domain of scientists.

Anthropology: the study of human societies by observing daily lives and customs, culture, and behavior, using methods drawn from the fields of social science and the sciences.

Basque: the name of the ancient race inhabiting both slopes of the western Pyrenees mountains dividing the countries of Spain and France, adjacent to the Bay of Biscay, who speak their own Basque language.

Capitalism: a system of economic management in which factories and other institutions needed to produce goods and services are owned by private individuals rather than government. Typically, these individuals run their organizations for profits and compete with each other.

Charivaris: a French folk custom, part of which sees the local community gather outside the home of newly-weds the morning after the wedding and bang on pots and pans in a mock celebration of their marriage and fertility.

Civil Rights Movement: a social movement in the United States beginning in the 1950s that aimed to end discrimination in all its forms against black Americans. It began with protests over segregation in education and brought about the passing of laws confirming that white and black people had equal rights under the US Constitution.

Colonization: the process by which European nations such as France and Britain took control of countries in Africa, Asia, and the Middle East, and ruled them as colonies.

Communist: a follower of communism, a political ideology that relies on the state ownership of the means of production, the collectivization of labor, and the abolition of social class.

Companion of the Order of Canada: the second-highest public recognition for Canadian citizens who have contributed to public life, often by long endeavors throughout their careers. Appointments to the order come from the monarch of Canada, currently Her Majesty Queen Elizabeth II.

Cultural history: the study by historians of past cultures: the way in which social groups—villages, towns, cities, whole countries or areas of the globe—interact among themselves and without outsiders. Typical cultural histories focus on social customs, language conventions, rituals, and religions to recreate past people's cultures.

Cultural integration: the process by which people adjust their language, behavior, and customs in order to become part of social groups or society.

Cultural turn: a generalized shift in attention across the humanities, away from a scientific understanding of societies past and present toward an understanding of them in terms of individuals, groups, and customs. Beginning in the 1970s, the turn also had a political dimension, trying to democratize knowledge and research, to make it accessible to all and to cover the past lives of everyone, irrespective of gender, race, or class.

Early-modern period: the period of history beginning with the end of the Middle Ages in around 1500 and ending with the French Revolution and Industrial Revolution, which are commonly understood to found the modern period in history in which we currently live.

Ethnography: the study of the people's place in a culture. Rather than studying cultures in the abstract, ethnographers look at a culture as perceived by an individual operating as part of that culture.

Ethnology: the branch of anthropology that compares and contrasts the particular characteristics of one society or tribe with those of another, with the aim of deepening human understanding of other ways of living and of human beings generally.

Global history: a field of study that seeks to heighten history's relevance today by comparing and contrasting the history of social, economic, and political practices in different parts of the world, rather than in one country.

Huguenots: individuals in France who committed themselves to the Protestant Church between 1550 and 1590. The Protestant Church sought to reform the Catholic Church by reducing the number and the intricacy of symbols and forms of worship involved in masses. Protestants also placed Bible study at the center of faith, an emphasis that did not exist in Catholicism.

Jewish: a word used to describe anything related to Jews and their cultural, religious, and social practices. Jews originated in Israel and the near east, and practice the religion of Judaism.

Marshall Plan: a four-year plan between 1948 and 1952 as part of which the American government gave $17 billion to European governments to help them rebuild their countries following World War II. With the plan came commitments from European governments to promote free trade between themselves and the United States.

Marxism: an approach to historical study or any other pursuit based on Marxism and the writings and methods of German philosopher Karl Marx (1818–83) which found events in all aspects of life to be the result of economic forces that determine human behavior.

McCarthy era: period between 1950 and 1956 when Republican Senator Joseph McCarthy encouraged and oversaw an era of political repression in America. Individuals accused of sympathizing with communism and/or the Soviet Union during the Cold War were often investigated by the government or private groups to make sure they were loyal to the US.

Microhistory: an approach to history that advocates intensively studying a small unit of analysis, such as an individual, a village, or a single group of people, in order to master the whole details of the subject. As a next phase, specific features of the study are often taken as informing more general questions regarding the individual's class, region, country, or society.

9/11 attacks: four attacks on the United States staged on September 11, 2001 and coordinated by the Islamist terrorist group al-Qaeda. The attacks resulted in almost 3,000 deaths.

Postmodernism: a view held by some historians and academics after the 1970s that modern approaches to history did not explain the past convincingly. People who follow the ideas of postmodernism believe that using scientific tools and other traditional means of understanding the world is not effective an way to relate past events to contemporary readers. Instead, postmodernists focus on the under-represented in society, such as women and ethnic minorities, and sexuality.

Progressive history/new history: a new approach to historical study, pioneered in the 1920s by American historians, that urged scholars to examine the lives and times of ordinary people using the latest techniques in economic and social research. This included a focus on revealing how society had determined the course of history. The approach is also referred to as progressive history, because scholars expressed a commitment to social reform in America and called themselves "progressive historians."

Protestantism/Protestant: a member of any of the Christian Churches or bodies that refuse to accept the Pope as head of the Church. Protestantism separated from Roman Catholicism in Europe during the Reformation.

Reformation: a movement that began in Europe around 1517 when Martin Luther nailed his 95 Theses to the door of a church in Wittenberg, Germany. It consisted of arguments over the teachings and practices of the Roman Catholic Church and a separated, reformed Church. The Protestant Church emerged during the sixteenth century.

Renaissance: a movement beginning in fourteenth-century Europe and ending in the seventeenth century. It witnessed the rise of educational and scholarly reform across Europe, leading to new techniques in art, the use of Latin in scholarship, laboratory experimentation in science, and the formulation of legal and diplomatic conventions.

Le Retour de Martin Guerre: a film version of the traditional story of Martin Guerre, directed by Daniel Vigne and released in 1982. Natalie Zemon Davis was the historical consultant on the movie.

Roman Catholic Church: one of the oldest remaining religious organizations, based in Rome in the Vatican City, headed by the Pope, and extending across the world by virtue of Roman Catholic churches found globally.

Rule of law: a legal and political doctrine that society must conduct itself in accordance with the laws passed by the legislature of a country, whether a House of Representatives or a parliament. In turn, government and citizens must abide by the law. **Self-fashioning:** the process by which people construct an image of themselves to present to people around them in accordance with social and cultural norms.

Socialism: the belief that society should be organized in such a way that the methods of production, distribution, and exchange are owned and regulated by the community as a whole, rather than by the select few..

Student movement: a series of student-led protests in the 1960s and culminating in demonstrations across the West in 1968, during which student groups led a campaign for greater academic freedom and student input in the governance of universities.

Subaltern studies: a sub-field of the humanities in general, including anthropology, ethnography, geography, history, and sociology, that seeks to look at the lives and times of peoples in Southeast Asia and other areas once subject to European colonial rule. The purpose of scholars in subaltern studies is to examine formerly colonized peoples on their own terms, not by imposing European and Western notions of modernization.

Surinam: the coastal region of South America between the Orinoco and Amazon rivers colonized by different European powers since around 1600. In the eighteenth century it was subject to British rule.

Third World: the term now used generally for the developing countries of Africa, Asia, and Latin America. It was originally used post-World War II to describe those countries not aligned with either the US or USSR during the Cold War.

United Nations: an organization with headquarters in New York City designed to foster co-operation between governments around the world. It was set up in 1945 following World War II and plays an important role in promoting world peace and responding to human and natural disasters.

US Supreme Court: the highest court in America that hears appeals from federal courts, as well as providing authoritative judgments on all matters of constitutional law.

Women's Liberation Movement: a movement in America, formed by associations between women and men to improve women's personal, professional, and civil rights. The movement gained support in the 1960s and into the 1970s when it campaigned for equality between men and women.

World War II: a worldwide, armed conflict lasting from 1939 until 1945. The German invasion of Poland began the conflict and America entered the war in December 1941 when Germany's ally Japan attacked a US naval base at Pearl Harbor.

PEOPLE MENTIONED IN THE TEXT

Johannes Leo Africanus (c. 1494–c. 1554) was a Muslim, Arabic-speaking Egyptian diplomat and author, known for his *Descrittione dell'Africa* ("Description of Africa").

Frank Ankersmit (b. 1945) is a retired Dutch professor of intellectual history. He considers the role of reality and text in how historians convey truth and meaning about the past, which is the focus of his book, *Meaning, Truth and Reference in Historical Representation* (2012).

Charles Beard (1874–1948) was an American historian of US society and politics. He is best known for his reading of the American constitution as an act of economic self-interest: *An Economic Interpretation of the Constitution of the United States* (1913).

Marc Bloch (1886–1944) was a French medieval historian, founder of the *Annales* school,★ and member of the French Resistance, who fought to obstruct German occupation of France during World War II.

Daniel Boorstin (1914–2004) was an American historian of American and world history and librarian to the United States Congress. His work *The Image: A Guide to Pseudo-Events in America* (1961) gave rise to what historians now identify as postmodernism.

Susan Broomhall is a professor at the University of Western Australia specializing in the history of emotions, women's history, and early modern violence.

Peter Burke (b. 1937) is a British historian of European history, currently Emeritus Professor of Cultural History and fellow of Emmanuel College, Cambridge. Burke is a firm proponent of cultural history, to which his book *What is Cultural History* (2004) is a useful introduction.

Richard Burt is professor of English literature at the University of Florida. His research interests cover early-modern literature and media.

Dipesh Chakrabarty (b. 1948) is a Bengali historian of Southeast Asia, currently Lawrence A. Kimpton Distinguished Service Professor of History, South Asian Languages and Civilizations and the College at the University of Chicago in the United States. He is best known for his book *Provincializing Europe: Postcolonial Thought and Historical Difference*.

Rosalie Colie (1924–72) was an American literature scholar, professor of comparative literature, and first woman chair of the English Literature Department at Brown University in 1972.

R. G. Collingwood (1889–1943) was an English philosopher and historian who was Waynfleete Professor of Metaphysical Philosophy at Magdalene College, Oxford. His most famous book is *The Idea of History* (1946) in which he argues that history enables readers to re-enact the past as they read.

Jean de Coras (1515–72) was a judge and legal scholar in southern France. He was a judge at the trial of Arnaud du Tilh and wrote a published account of the proceedings. Davis used that account for her research for *The Return of Martin Guerre*.

Chandler Davis (b. 1926) is an American-Canadian mathematician and husband of Natalie Zemon Davis. His career began in Canada in the 1960s and he has also written science fiction.

Barbara Diefendorf (b. 1949) is an American historian of France and Europe, who has spent most of her career at Boston University, where she is currently a professor. Her most recent book is *The Saint Bartholomew's Day Massacre: A Brief History with Documents* (2008).

Lucien Febvre (1878–1956) was a French historian of French and European economic and social history, and a founding member of the *Annales* school with Marc Bloch. Like Davis, Febvre studied the popular religious beliefs, politics, economics, and society of sixteenth-century France and is perhaps best known for *Le Problème de l'Incroyance: La Religion de Rabelais* ("The Problem of Unbelief: The Religion of Rabelais").

Robert Finlay (b. 1953) is an American historian of sixteenth-century Italy, and currently professor in the Department of Theology at the University of Arkansas. He was one of the harshest critics of Davis's *The Return of Martin Guerre*.

Clifford Geertz (1926–2006) was an American anthropologist who dominated the discipline at the end of the twentieth century and worked as a professor at the Centre for Advanced Studies, Princeton. His most famous work is *The Interpretation of Cultures* (1973).

Carlo Ginzburg (b. 1939) is an Italian historian of early-modern Europe and the Reformation, noted for placing his historical topics in an interdisciplinary framework using a variety of sources, from art to scientific manuals. He is best known for *The Cheese and the Worms* (1980), which was originally published in Italy as *Il Formaggio e i Vermi* in 1976.

Henri Hauser (1866–1946) was a French historian whose work focused on medieval and early-modern history and economic history. His best known works focus on economic history and its role in explaining political and economic crises current in his lifetime.

Carla Hesse (b. 1956) is an American historian of France, and Peder Sather Professor of History at the University of California at Berkeley. Among her best-known books is *The Other Enlightenment: How French Women Became Modern* (2001).

Lynn Hunt (b. 1945) is an American historian of France and global history, who is currently Eugen Weber Professor of Modern History at the University of California, Los Angeles. She specializes in the history of the French, gender, and world history as demonstrated by her widely used textbook *The Making of the West: Peoples and Cultures*.

W. K. Jordan (1902–80) was an American historian of sixteenth- and seventeenth-century Britain. He became an authority on English history.

Joan Kelly (1928–82) was an American historian of the Italian Renaissance. Her famous article "Did Women Have a Renaissance?" argued that women's power and their ability to control events actually diminished during the Renaissance, when bourgeois literature set the standard image of women as dependent on men.

Dorothy Ko is professor of history at Barnard College, part of the City University of New York. She specializes in the history of women, gender, and material cultures in early-modern China.

Emmanuel Le Roy Ladurie (b. 1929) is a French historian of France during the early-modern period with a particular interest in the French peasantry. Ladurie wrote histories of the lower orders such as *Les Paysans de Languedoc* ("The Peasants of Languedoc").

Janet Lewis (1889–1998) was an American novelist and poet who studied literature at the University of Chicago and later taught it at Stanford and the University of California at Berkeley. Lewis wrote about the story of Martin Guerre in *The Wife of Martin Guerre* (1941).

Menocchio (unknown–1599) was also known as Domenico de Scandella, a miller from Montereale, Italy. He was burned at the stake on the orders of Pope Clement VIII for dissenting from Catholic Church doctrine.

Michel de Montaigne (1533–92) was a French philosopher of the Renaissance who became famous for his use of essays to make philosophical points. His *Essais* of 1580 remain his best-known works, and in the essay "On the Lame" he discusses the verdict in the Martin Guerre case in 1560.

Andronicus Tranquillus Parthenius (1490–1571) was a Croatian scholar whose works commented extensively on developments in Renaissance Europe.

David Potter is Emeritus Reader in History at the University of Kent, UK. His work focuses on early-modern French history.

James Harvey Robinson (1863–1936) was an American historian of American and European history and specialist in historical method. His work promoted the new history, examining the condition of ordinary Americans throughout the past, highlighting the need for present social reform as in his collection of essays *The New History* (1912).

Peter Sahlins (b. 1957) is an American historian of France, who is currently professor of history at the University of California at Berkeley. He founded the University of California Paris Study Centre and one of his latest works is *Unnaturally French: Foreign Citizens in the Old Regime and After* (2004).

Arthur Meier Schlesinger Jr. (1917–2007) was an American historian who worked on the history of the Democratic Party and was both a professional historian and New York socialite for his whole career. He wrote political histories such as *A Thousand Days: John F. Kennedy in the White House* (1965) and *The Crisis of Confidence* (1973).

Bonnie G. Smith is Board of Governors Distinguished Professor of History at Rutgers University, New Brunswick, New Jersey, and a specialist in women's and gender history and theory. Her work promotes awareness of under-represented women and female groups and their contributions to the world as in her introductory volume, *Women's Studies: Basic Concepts* (2013).

Lawrence Stone (1919–99) was a British historian of early-modern Britain, focusing on the English Civil War (1642–51), family history, and class identity. From 1963 until 1990 he was Dodge Professor of History at Princeton where Natalie Zemon Davis also worked.

Joseph R. Strayer (1904–87) was an American historian of the Crusades and medieval Europe, who chaired the history department at Princeton University between 1941 and 1961. His published work includes *The Reign of Philip the Fair* (1980).

Palmer Throop (1901–86) was an American historian of medieval Europe, in particular the Crusades. He studied popular religious beliefs in Europe, as well as papal history, and ran an innovative graduate class on the role of gender in medieval society into the 1950s.

Hayden White (b. 1928) is an American historian of literature and literary criticism. His best-known work is *Metahistory: The Historical Imagination in Nineteenth-Century Europe* (1973).

Howard Zinn (1922–2010) was an American historian and social reformer who worked at Boston University and Spelman College. He specialized in the social history of the lower classes in America.

WORKS CITED

WORKS CITED

Adelson, Roger. "Interview with Natalie Zemon Davis." *Historian* 53 (1991): 405–22.

Agnew, Jean-Christophe. "Capitalism, Culture and Catastrophe." In *The Cultural Turn in US History: Past, Present & Future,* edited by James W. Cook and Lawrence B. Glickman, 383–415. Chicago: University of Chicago Press, 2008.

Anderssen, Erin. "The Order of Canada: An Accolade that Demonstrates Why Waving the Flag Just Isn't Enough." *The Globe and Mail,* June 30, 2012. Accessed April 23, 2015. http://www.theglobeandmail.com/news/national/the-order-of-canada-an-accolade-that-demonstrates-why-waving-the-flag-just-isnt-enough/article4382059/?page=all.

Ankersmit, Frank. *The Reality Effect in the Writing of History: The Dynamics of Historiographical Topology.* Amsterdam: Noord-Hollandsche, 1989.

Atwood, Bain, Dipesh Chakrabarty, and Claudio Lomnitz. "The Public Life of History." *Public Culture* 20 (2015). http://publicculture.org/articles/view/20/1/the-public-life-of-history.

Azzolini, Monica, and Martyn Lyons. "Natalie Zemon Davis: An E-Mail Interview with Martyn Lyons and Monica Azzolini." *History Australia* 2 (2005): 91.1–91.10.

Bancroft, George. *History of the United States from the Discovery of the American Continent.* 6 vols. Boston, MA: Little and Brown, 1834.

Beard, Charles and James Harvey Robinson. *History of Europe, Our Own Times: The Eighteenth and Nineteenth Centuries, the Opening of the Twentieth Century, The World War and Recent Events.* Boston, MA: Ginn, 1932.

Beard, Charles, and Alfred Vagts. "Currents of Thought in Historiography." *American Historical Review* 42 (1937): 460–83.

Benedict, Philip. "Between Whig Traditions and New Histories: American Historical Writing about Reformation and Early Modern Europe." In *Imagined Histories: American Historians Interpret the Past*, edited by Anthony Molho and Gordon S. Wood, 295–323. Princeton, NJ: Princeton University Press, 1998.

Benson, Edward. "The Look of the Past: *Le Retour de Martin Guerre.*" *Radical History Review* 28 (1984): 125–30.

Bentley, Jerry H. *Old World Encounters: Cross-Cultural Contacts and Exchanges in Pre-Modern Times.* Oxford: Oxford University Press, 1993.

Bentley, Michael. "Reflecting on the Modern Age." In *Companion to Historiography,* edited by Michael Bentley, 395–508. London: Routledge, 1999.

Best, Steven. "Cultural Turn." In *Blackwell Encyclopedia of Sociology*, edited by George Ritzer, 177. Oxford: Blackwell, 2007.

Bhattacharya, Sabyasachi. "History from Below." *Social Scientist* 11 (1983): 3–20.

Bienen, Leigh Buchanan. "The Law as Storyteller: *The Return of Martin Guerre* by Natalie Zemon Davis." *Harvard Law Review* 98 (1984): 494–502.

Biggs, Melissa E. *French Films, 1945–1993*. Jefferson, NC: McFarland, 1993.

Breisach, Ernst A. *American Progressive History: An Experiment in Modernization*. Chicago: University of Chicago Press, 1993.

Broomhall, Susan. *Women and Religion in Sixteenth-Century France*. Basingstoke: Palgrave Macmillan, 2005.

Brown, Peter. *The Making of Late Antiquity*. Cambridge, MA: Harvard University Press, 1976.

Burgière, André. *The Annales School: An Intellectual History*. Translated by Jane Marie Todd. Ithaca, NY: Cornell University Press, 2009.

Burrow, John. *A History of Histories*. London: Allen Lane 2007.

Buzan, Barry, and George Lawson. *The Global Transformation: History, Modernity and the Making of International Relations*. Cambridge: Cambridge University Press, 2015.

Chakrabarty, Dipesh. *Provincializing Europe: Postcolonial Thought and Historical Difference*. Princeton, NJ: Princeton University Press, 2000.

"Subaltern Studies and Postcolonial Historiography." *Nepantla: Views from South* 1 (2000): 9–32.

Chaunu, Pierre, and Huguette Chaunu. *Séville et l'Atlantique (1504–1560)* ("Seville and the Atlantic"). 12 vols. Paris: Hachette, 1955–9.

Collingwood, R. G. *The Idea of History*. Oxford: Oxford University Press, 1946.

Cook, James W., and Lawrence B. Glickman. "Twelve Propositions for a History of US Cultural History." In *The Cultural Turn in US History: Past, Present & Future,* edited by James W. Cook and Lawrence B. Glickman, 3–58. Chicago: University of Chicago Press, 2008.

Davis, Natalie Zemon. *Society and Culture in Early Modern France: Eight Essays*. Stanford, CA: Stanford University Press, 1975.

"Ghosts, Kin and Progeny: Some Features of Family Life in Early Modern France." *Daedalus* 106 (1977): 87–114.

Anthropology and History in the 1980s: The Possibilities of the Past." *Journal of Interdisciplinary History* 12 (1981): 267–75.

The Return of Martin Guerre. Cambridge MA: Harvard University Press, 1983.

Frauen und Gesellschaft am Beginn der Neuzeit ("Women and Society at the Outset of Modernity"). Berlin: Wagenbach 1986.

"Any Resemblance to Persons Living or Dead: Film and the Challenge to Authenticity." *Yale Review* 86 (1987): 457–82.

Fiction in the Archives. Pardon Tales and Their Tellers in Sixteenth-Century France. Stanford, CA: Stanford University Press, 1987.

"Fame and Secrecy: Leon Modena's Life as an Early Modern Autobiography." *History and Theory* 27 (1988): 103–18.

"History's Two Bodies." *American Historical Review* 93 (1988): 1–30.

"On the Lame," *American Historical Review* 93 (1988): 572–603.

Gender in the Academy: Women and Learning from Plato to Princeton. An Exhibition Celebrating the 20th Anniversary of Undergraduate Co-Education at Princeton University. Princeton, NJ: Princeton University Press, 1990.

"Stories and the Hunger to Know." *Yale Journal of Criticism* 5 (1992): 159–63.

Women on the Margins: Three Seventeenth Century Lives. Cambridge, MA: Harvard University Press, 1995.

A Life of Learning. New York: American Council of Learned Societies, 1997.

Remaking Imposters: From Martin Guerre to Sommersby. Hayes Robinson Lecture Series no. 1. Egham: Royal Holloway Publications Unit, 1997.

"Movie or Monograph? A Historian/Filmmaker's Perspective." *Public Historian* 25 (2003): 45–8.

Trickster Travels: In Search of Leo Africanus, A Muslim Between Worlds. London: Faber, 2006.

A Passion for History: Conversations with Denis Crouzet. Kirksville, MO: Truman State University Press, 2010.

"Why Gender and Women's Studies Matters: Carla Hesse Interviews Natalie Zemon Davis." *Medievalists.net,* October 10, 2010. Accessed April 23, 2015. http://www.medievalists.net/2010/10/10/natalie-zemon-davis-why-gender-and-womens-studies-matter/.

"Decentering History: Local Stories and Global Crossings in a Global World." *History and Theory* 50 (2011): 188–202.

"What is Universal About History?" In *Transnationale Geschichte: Themen, Tendenzen und Theorien*, edited by Gunilla Budde, Sebastian Conrad, and Oliver Janz, 15–20. Göttingen: Vandenhoeck & Ruprecht, 2011.

"David Nassy's Furlough and the Slave Mattheas." In *New Essays in American Jewish History Commemorating the Sixtieth Anniversary of the Founding of the Jewish Archives,* edited by Pamela Nadell, 79–94. Cincinatti, OH: American Jewish Archives, 2012.Dewald, Jonathan. "Fiction in the Archives. Pardon Tales and Their Tellers in Sixteenth-Century France (Book Review)." *Journal of Social History* 22 (1989): 767–9.

Diefendorf, Barbara B. *The Saint Bartholomew's Day Massacre: A Brief History with Documents*. Boston: St. Martin's, 2008.

Diefendorf, Barbara B., and Carla Hesse. *Culture and Identity in Early Modern Europe (1500–1800): Essays in Honor of Natalie Zemon Davis*. Ann Arbor, MI: Michigan University Press, 1993.

Elias, Christine. "Natalie Zemon Davis Receives National Humanities Medal: Renowned Adjunct Professor of History Honored." *University of Toronto News*. Accessed April 23, 2015. http://news.utoronto.ca/natalie-zemon-davis-receives-national-humanities-medal.

Fabre, Daniel. "Review of *The Return of Martin Guerre*." *Annales. Histoire, Sciences Sociales* 41 (1986): 708–11.

Finlay, Robert. *Politics in Renaissance Venice*. London: Ernest Benn, 1980.

"The Refashioning of Martin Guerre." *American Historical Review* 93 (1988): 553–71.

Friedrichs, Christopher R. "Review of *Society and Culture in Early Modern France*." *Sixteenth Century Journal* 40 (2009): 68–70.

Geertz, Clifford. "Thick Description: Toward an Interpretive Theory of Cultures." In Clifford Geertz, *The Interpretation of Cultures*. New York: Perseus, 1973.

Ginzburg, Carlo. *The Cheese and the Worms: The Cosmos of a Sixteenth-Century Miller*. Baltimore, MD: Johns Hopkins University Press, 1980.

Greenblatt, Stephen J. *Renaissance Self-Fashioning: From More to Shakespeare*. Chicago: University of Chicago Press, 1980.

Grossberg, Lawrence. "Cultural Studies: What's in a Name (One More Time)." *Journal of Education and Culture* 1 (1995): 1–37.

Halttunnen, Karen. "The Art of Listening." In *The Cultural Turn in US History: Past, Present & Future,* edited by James W. Cook and Lawrence B. Glickman, 417–24. Chicago: University of Chicago Press, 2008.

Harding, Rob. "Interview with Natalie Zemon Davis." In *Visions of History*, edited by Henry Abelove, Betsy Blackmar, Peter Dimock, and Jonathan Schneer, 99–122. Manchester: Manchester University Press, 1983.

Hesse, Carla. *The Other Enlightenment: How French Women Became Modern*. Princeton, NJ: Princeton University Press, 2001.

Hesse, Carla, and Peter Sahlins. "Mobility in France." Special issue of *French Historical Studies* 29 (2006).

Hexter, Jack. *Doing History*. Bloomington, IN: Indiana University Press, 1968.

Higham, John. *History: Professional Scholarship in America*. Baltimore, MD: Johns Hopkins University Press, 1965.

Hughes-Warrington, Marnie. *Fifty Key Thinkers on History*. London: Routledge, 2000.

Hunt, Lynn. "History, Culture, Text." In *The New Cultural History*, edited by Lynn Hunt, 1–23. Berkeley, CA: California University Press, 1989.

Writing History in a Global Era. Boston: W. W. Norton & Company, 2014.

Iggers, Georg. *Historiography: From Scientific Objectivity to the Postmodern Challenge*. Middletown, CT: Wesleyan University Press, 1997.

Kelley, Donald R. "Review of *The Return of Martin Guerre*." *Renaissance Quarterly* 37 (1984): 252.

Kelly, Joan. "Did Women Have a Renaissance?" In *Becoming Visible: Women in European History*, edited by Renate Bridenthal and Claudia Koonz, 137–64. Boston: Houghton Mifflin, 1977.

Knecht, Robert J. "Review of the *Return of Martin Guerre*." *History* 70 (1985): 121.

Ladurie, Emmanuel Le Roy. *Les Paysans de Languedoc* (*The Peasants of Languedoc*). 2 vols. Paris: SEVPEN, 1966.

Montaillou: Village Occitan de 1294 à 1324 ("Montaillou: Languedoc Village from 1294 until 1324"). Paris: Gallimard, 1975.

"Review of *The Return of Martin Guerre*." *New York Review of Books*, December 30, 1983.

Lebovics, Herman. *Bringing the Empire Back Home: France in a Global Age*. Durham, NC: Duke University Press, 2004.

Lewis, Janet. *The Wife of Martin Guerre*. Athens, OH: Ohio University Press, 1943.

Liu, Lydia H., Rebecca E. Karl, and Dorothy Ko, eds. *The Birth of Chinese*

Feminism: Essential Texts in Transnational Theory. New York: Columbia University Press, 2013.

Miller, Susan Gilson. "Review of *Trickster Travels: In Search of Leo Africanus, A Sixteenth-Century Muslim Between Worlds*." *Journal of Interdisciplinary History* 38 (2007): 261–4.

Monter, William. "Review of *The Return of Martin Guerre*." *Sixteenth Century Journal* 14 (1983): 516.

Moote, A. Lloyd. "Review of *The Return of Martin Guerre*." *American Historical Review* 90 (1985): 943.

Novick, Peter. *That Noble Dream: The "Objectivity Question" and the American Historical Profession*. Cambridge: Cambridge University Press, 1988.

Partner, Nancy, and Sarah Foot, eds. *The Sage Handbook of Historical Theory*. London: Routledge, 2013.

Perl-Rosenthal, Nathan. "Comment: Generational Turns." *American Historical Review* 117 (2012): 804–12.

Rabel, Robert J. "Impersonation and Identity: *Sommersby, The Return of Martin Guerre,* and the *Odyssey*." *International Journal of Classical Tradition* 9 (2003): 391–406.

Robinson, James Harvey. *The New History: Essays Illustrating the Modern Historical Outlook*. New York: Macmillan, 1911.

Rodgers, Daniel T. *Age of Fracture*. Cambridge, MA: Harvard University Press, 2011.

Rublack, Ulinka, ed. *A Concise Companion to History*. Oxford: Oxford University Press, 2011.

Sahlins, Peter. "Deep Play in the Forests: The 'War of Demoiselles' in the Ariège, 1829–31." In *Culture and Identity in Early Modern Europe (1500–1800): Essays in Honor of Natalie Zemon Davis*, 159–79. Ann Arbor, MI: Michigan University Press, 1993.

Unnaturally French: Foreign Citizens in the Old Regime and After. Ithaca, NY: Cornell University Press, 2004.

Schlesinger, Arthur Meier, Jr. *A Life in the Twentieth Century: Innocent Beginnings, 1917–1950.* New York: Mariner, 2002.

Scott, Joan. "Storytelling," *History and Theory* 50 (2011): 203–9.

Smith, Bonnie G. *The Gender of History: Men, Women and Historical Practice*. Cambridge, MA: Harvard University Press, 1998.

Stewart, John Hall. "Beatrice Fry Hyslop: A Tribute." *French Historical Studies* 7 (1972): 473–8.

Stone, Lawrence. "The Revival of Narrative: Reflections on a New Old History." *Past and Present* 85 (1979): 3–24.

Strayer, Joseph R. "Feudalism in Western Europe." In *Feudalism in History*, edited by Rushton Coulborn. Princeton, NJ: Princeton University Press, 1956.

Thernstrom, Stephan. *Poverty and Progress: Social Mobility in a Nineteenth-Century City.* Cambridge, MA: Harvard University Press, 1964.

Tindall, George Brown, and David Emory Shi. *America: A Narrative History*. New York: W. W. Norton & Company, 2007.

White, Hayden. *Metahistory: The Historical Imagination of Nineteenth-Century Europe*. Baltimore, MD: Johns Hopkins University Press, 1973.

THE MACAT LIBRARY
BY DISCIPLINE

AFRICANA STUDIES

Chinua Achebe's *An Image of Africa: Racism in Conrad's Heart of Darkness*
W. E. B. Du Bois's *The Souls of Black Folk*
Zora Neale Huston's *Characteristics of Negro Expression*
Martin Luther King Jr's *Why We Can't Wait*
Toni Morrison's *Playing in the Dark: Whiteness in the American Literary Imagination*

ANTHROPOLOGY

Arjun Appadurai's *Modernity at Large: Cultural Dimensions of Globalisation*
Philippe Ariès's *Centuries of Childhood*
Franz Boas's *Race, Language and Culture*
Kim Chan & Renée Mauborgne's *Blue Ocean Strategy*
Jared Diamond's *Guns, Germs & Steel: the Fate of Human Societies*
Jared Diamond's *Collapse: How Societies Choose to Fail or Survive*
E. E. Evans-Pritchard's *Witchcraft, Oracles and Magic Among the Azande*
James Ferguson's *The Anti-Politics Machine*
Clifford Geertz's *The Interpretation of Cultures*
David Graeber's *Debt: the First 5000 Years*
Karen Ho's *Liquidated: An Ethnography of Wall Street*
Geert Hofstede's *Culture's Consequences: Comparing Values, Behaviors, Institutes and Organizations across Nations*
Claude Lévi-Strauss's *Structural Anthropology*
Jay Macleod's *Ain't No Makin' It: Aspirations and Attainment in a Low-Income Neighborhood*
Saba Mahmood's *The Politics of Piety: The Islamic Revival and the Feminist Subject*
Marcel Mauss's *The Gift*

BUSINESS

Jean Lave & Etienne Wenger's *Situated Learning*
Theodore Levitt's *Marketing Myopia*
Burton G. Malkiel's *A Random Walk Down Wall Street*
Douglas McGregor's *The Human Side of Enterprise*
Michael Porter's *Competitive Strategy: Creating and Sustaining Superior Performance*
John Kotter's *Leading Change*
C. K. Prahalad & Gary Hamel's *The Core Competence of the Corporation*

CRIMINOLOGY

Michelle Alexander's *The New Jim Crow: Mass Incarceration in the Age of Colorblindness*
Michael R. Gottfredson & Travis Hirschi's *A General Theory of Crime*
Richard Herrnstein & Charles A. Murray's *The Bell Curve: Intelligence and Class Structure in American Life*
Elizabeth Loftus's *Eyewitness Testimony*
Jay Macleod's *Ain't No Makin' It: Aspirations and Attainment in a Low-Income Neighborhood*
Philip Zimbardo's *The Lucifer Effect*

ECONOMICS

Janet Abu-Lughod's *Before European Heqemony*
Ha-Joon Chang's *Kicking Away the Ladder*
David Brion Davis's *The Problem of Slavery in the Age of Revolution*
Milton Friedman's *The Role of Monetary Policy*
Milton Friedman's *Capitalism and Freedom*
David Graeber's *Debt: the First 5000 Years*
Friedrich Hayek's *The Road to Serfdom*
Karen Ho's *Liquidated: An Ethnography of Wall Street*

John Maynard Keynes's *The General Theory of Employment, Interest and Money*
Charles P. Kindleberger's *Manias, Panics and Crashes*
Robert Lucas's *Why Doesn't Capital Flow from Rich to Poor Countries?*
Burton G. Malkiel's *A Random Walk Down Wall Street*
Thomas Robert Malthus's *An Essay on the Principle of Population*
Karl Marx's *Capital*
Thomas Piketty's *Capital in the Twenty-First Century*
Amartya Sen's *Development as Freedom*
Adam Smith's *The Wealth of Nations*
Nassim Nicholas Taleb's *The Black Swan: The Impact of the Highly Improbable*
Amos Tversky's & Daniel Kahneman's *Judgment under Uncertainty: Heuristics and Biases*
Mahbub Ul Haq's *Reflections on Human Development*
Max Weber's *The Protestant Ethic and the Spirit of Capitalism*

FEMINISM AND GENDER STUDIES

Judith Butler's *Gender Trouble*
Simone De Beauvoir's *The Second Sex*
Michel Foucault's *History of Sexuality*
Betty Friedan's *The Feminine Mystique*
Saba Mahmood's *The Politics of Piety: The Islamic Revival and the Feminist Subject*
Joan Wallach Scott's *Gender and the Politics of History*
Mary Wollstonecraft's *A Vindication of the Rights of Woman*
Virginia Woolf's *A Room of One's Own*

GEOGRAPHY

The Brundtland Report's *Our Common Future*
Rachel Carson's *Silent Spring*
Charles Darwin's *On the Origin of Species*
James Ferguson's *The Anti-Politics Machine*
Jane Jacobs's *The Death and Life of Great American Cities*
James Lovelock's *Gaia: A New Look at Life on Earth*
Amartya Sen's *Development as Freedom*
Mathis Wackernagel & William Rees's *Our Ecological Footprint*

HISTORY

Janet Abu-Lughod's *Before European Hegemony*
Benedict Anderson's *Imagined Communities*
Bernard Bailyn's *The Ideological Origins of the American Revolution*
Hanna Batatu's *The Old Social Classes And The Revolutionary Movements Of Iraq*
Christopher Browning's *Ordinary Men: Reserve Police Batallion 101 and the Final Solution in Poland*
Edmund Burke's *Reflections on the Revolution in France*
William Cronon's *Nature's Metropolis: Chicago And The Great West*
Alfred W. Crosby's *The Columbian Exchange*
Hamid Dabashi's *Iran: A People Interrupted*
David Brion Davis's *The Problem of Slavery in the Age of Revolution*
Nathalie Zemon Davis's *The Return of Martin Guerre*
Jared Diamond's *Guns, Germs & Steel: the Fate of Human Societies*
Frank Dikotter's *Mao's Great Famine*
John W Dower's *War Without Mercy: Race And Power In The Pacific War*
W. E. B. Du Bois's *The Souls of Black Folk*
Richard J. Evans's *In Defence of History*
Lucien Febvre's *The Problem of Unbelief in the 16th Century*
Sheila Fitzpatrick's *Everyday Stalinism*

Eric Foner's *Reconstruction: America's Unfinished Revolution, 1863-1877*
Michel Foucault's *Discipline and Punish*
Michel Foucault's *History of Sexuality*
Francis Fukuyama's *The End of History and the Last Man*
John Lewis Gaddis's *We Now Know: Rethinking Cold War History*
Ernest Gellner's *Nations and Nationalism*
Eugene Genovese's *Roll, Jordan, Roll: The World the Slaves Made*
Carlo Ginzburg's *The Night Battles*
Daniel Goldhagen's *Hitler's Willing Executioners*
Jack Goldstone's *Revolution and Rebellion in the Early Modern World*
Antonio Gramsci's *The Prison Notebooks*
Alexander Hamilton, John Jay & James Madison's *The Federalist Papers*
Christopher Hill's *The World Turned Upside Down*
Carole Hillenbrand's *The Crusades: Islamic Perspectives*
Thomas Hobbes's *Leviathan*
Eric Hobsbawm's *The Age Of Revolution*
John A. Hobson's *Imperialism: A Study*
Albert Hourani's *History of the Arab Peoples*
Samuel P. Huntington's *The Clash of Civilizations and the Remaking of World Order*
C. L. R. James's *The Black Jacobins*
Tony Judt's *Postwar: A History of Europe Since 1945*
Ernst Kantorowicz's *The King's Two Bodies: A Study in Medieval Political Theology*
Paul Kennedy's *The Rise and Fall of the Great Powers*
Ian Kershaw's *The "Hitler Myth": Image and Reality in the Third Reich*
John Maynard Keynes's *The General Theory of Employment, Interest and Money*
Charles P. Kindleberger's *Manias, Panics and Crashes*
Martin Luther King Jr's *Why We Can't Wait*
Henry Kissinger's *World Order: Reflections on the Character of Nations and the Course of History*
Thomas Kuhn's *The Structure of Scientific Revolutions*
Georges Lefebvre's *The Coming of the French Revolution*
John Locke's *Two Treatises of Government*
Niccolò Machiavelli's *The Prince*
Thomas Robert Malthus's *An Essay on the Principle of Population*
Mahmood Mamdani's *Citizen and Subject: Contemporary Africa And The Legacy Of Late Colonialism*
Karl Marx's *Capital*
Stanley Milgram's *Obedience to Authority*
John Stuart Mill's *On Liberty*
Thomas Paine's *Common Sense*
Thomas Paine's *Rights of Man*
Geoffrey Parker's *Global Crisis: War, Climate Change and Catastrophe in the Seventeenth Century*
Jonathan Riley-Smith's *The First Crusade and the Idea of Crusading*
Jean-Jacques Rousseau's *The Social Contract*
Joan Wallach Scott's *Gender and the Politics of History*
Theda Skocpol's *States and Social Revolutions*
Adam Smith's *The Wealth of Nations*
Timothy Snyder's *Bloodlands: Europe Between Hitler and Stalin*
Sun Tzu's *The Art of War*
Keith Thomas's *Religion and the Decline of Magic*
Thucydides's *The History of the Peloponnesian War*
Frederick Jackson Turner's *The Significance of the Frontier in American History*
Odd Arne Westad's *The Global Cold War: Third World Interventions And The Making Of Our Times*

LITERATURE

Chinua Achebe's *An Image of Africa: Racism in Conrad's Heart of Darkness*
Roland Barthes's *Mythologies*
Homi K. Bhabha's *The Location of Culture*
Judith Butler's *Gender Trouble*
Simone De Beauvoir's *The Second Sex*
Ferdinand De Saussure's *Course in General Linguistics*
T. S. Eliot's *The Sacred Wood: Essays on Poetry and Criticism*
Zora Neale Huston's *Characteristics of Negro Expression*
Toni Morrison's *Playing in the Dark: Whiteness in the American Literary Imagination*
Edward Said's *Orientalism*
Gayatri Chakravorty Spivak's *Can the Subaltern Speak?*
Mary Wollstonecraft's *A Vindication of the Rights of Women*
Virginia Woolf's *A Room of One's Own*

PHILOSOPHY

Elizabeth Anscombe's *Modern Moral Philosophy*
Hannah Arendt's *The Human Condition*
Aristotle's *Metaphysics*
Aristotle's *Nicomachean Ethics*
Edmund Gettier's *Is Justified True Belief Knowledge?*
Georg Wilhelm Friedrich Hegel's *Phenomenology of Spirit*
David Hume's *Dialogues Concerning Natural Religion*
David Hume's *The Enquiry for Human Understanding*
Immanuel Kant's *Religion within the Boundaries of Mere Reason*
Immanuel Kant's *Critique of Pure Reason*
Søren Kierkegaard's *The Sickness Unto Death*
Søren Kierkegaard's *Fear and Trembling*
C. S. Lewis's *The Abolition of Man*
Alasdair MacIntyre's *After Virtue*
Marcus Aurelius's *Meditations*
Friedrich Nietzsche's *On the Genealogy of Morality*
Friedrich Nietzsche's *Beyond Good and Evil*
Plato's *Republic*
Plato's *Symposium*
Jean-Jacques Rousseau's *The Social Contract*
Gilbert Ryle's *The Concept of Mind*
Baruch Spinoza's *Ethics*
Sun Tzu's *The Art of War*
Ludwig Wittgenstein's *Philosophical Investigations*

POLITICS

Benedict Anderson's *Imagined Communities*
Aristotle's *Politics*
Bernard Bailyn's *The Ideological Origins of the American Revolution*
Edmund Burke's *Reflections on the Revolution in France*
John C. Calhoun's *A Disquisition on Government*
Ha-Joon Chang's *Kicking Away the Ladder*
Hamid Dabashi's *Iran: A People Interrupted*
Hamid Dabashi's *Theology of Discontent: The Ideological Foundation of the Islamic Revolution in Iran*
Robert Dahl's *Democracy and its Critics*
Robert Dahl's *Who Governs?*
David Brion Davis's *The Problem of Slavery in the Age of Revolution*

Alexis De Tocqueville's *Democracy in America*
James Ferguson's *The Anti-Politics Machine*
Frank Dikotter's *Mao's Great Famine*
Sheila Fitzpatrick's *Everyday Stalinism*
Eric Foner's *Reconstruction: America's Unfinished Revolution, 1863-1877*
Milton Friedman's *Capitalism and Freedom*
Francis Fukuyama's *The End of History and the Last Man*
John Lewis Gaddis's *We Now Know: Rethinking Cold War History*
Ernest Gellner's *Nations and Nationalism*
David Graeber's *Debt: the First 5000 Years*
Antonio Gramsci's *The Prison Notebooks*
Alexander Hamilton, John Jay & James Madison's *The Federalist Papers*
Friedrich Hayek's *The Road to Serfdom*
Christopher Hill's *The World Turned Upside Down*
Thomas Hobbes's *Leviathan*
John A. Hobson's *Imperialism: A Study*
Samuel P. Huntington's *The Clash of Civilizations and the Remaking of World Order*
Tony Judt's *Postwar: A History of Europe Since 1945*
David C. Kang's *China Rising: Peace, Power and Order in East Asia*
Paul Kennedy's *The Rise and Fall of Great Powers*
Robert Keohane's *After Hegemony*
Martin Luther King Jr.'s *Why We Can't Wait*
Henry Kissinger's *World Order: Reflections on the Character of Nations and the Course of History*
John Locke's *Two Treatises of Government*
Niccolò Machiavelli's *The Prince*
Thomas Robert Malthus's *An Essay on the Principle of Population*
Mahmood Mamdani's *Citizen and Subject: Contemporary Africa And The Legacy Of
Late Colonialism*
Karl Marx's *Capital*
John Stuart Mill's *On Liberty*
John Stuart Mill's *Utilitarianism*
Hans Morgenthau's *Politics Among Nations*
Thomas Paine's *Common Sense*
Thomas Paine's *Rights of Man*
Thomas Piketty's *Capital in the Twenty-First Century*
Robert D. Putman's *Bowling Alone*
John Rawls's *Theory of Justice*
Jean-Jacques Rousseau's *The Social Contract*
Theda Skocpol's *States and Social Revolutions*
Adam Smith's *The Wealth of Nations*
Sun Tzu's *The Art of War*
Henry David Thoreau's *Civil Disobedience*
Thucydides's *The History of the Peloponnesian War*
Kenneth Waltz's *Theory of International Politics*
Max Weber's *Politics as a Vocation*
Odd Arne Westad's *The Global Cold War: Third World Interventions And The Making Of Our Times*

POSTCOLONIAL STUDIES

Roland Barthes's *Mythologies*
Frantz Fanon's *Black Skin, White Masks*
Homi K. Bhabha's *The Location of Culture*
Gustavo Gutiérrez's *A Theology of Liberation*
Edward Said's *Orientalism*
Gayatri Chakravorty Spivak's *Can the Subaltern Speak?*

The Macat Library By Discipline

PSYCHOLOGY

Gordon Allport's *The Nature of Prejudice*
Alan Baddeley & Graham Hitch's *Aggression: A Social Learning Analysis*
Albert Bandura's *Aggression: A Social Learning Analysis*
Leon Festinger's *A Theory of Cognitive Dissonance*
Sigmund Freud's *The Interpretation of Dreams*
Betty Friedan's *The Feminine Mystique*
Michael R. Gottfredson & Travis Hirschi's *A General Theory of Crime*
Eric Hoffer's *The True Believer: Thoughts on the Nature of Mass Movements*
William James's *Principles of Psychology*
Elizabeth Loftus's *Eyewitness Testimony*
A. H. Maslow's *A Theory of Human Motivation*
Stanley Milgram's *Obedience to Authority*
Steven Pinker's *The Better Angels of Our Nature*
Oliver Sacks's *The Man Who Mistook His Wife For a Hat*
Richard Thaler & Cass Sunstein's *Nudge: Improving Decisions About Health, Wealth and Happiness*
Amos Tversky's *Judgment under Uncertainty: Heuristics and Biases*
Philip Zimbardo's *The Lucifer Effect*

SCIENCE

Rachel Carson's *Silent Spring*
William Cronon's *Nature's Metropolis: Chicago And The Great West*
Alfred W. Crosby's *The Columbian Exchange*
Charles Darwin's *On the Origin of Species*
Richard Dawkin's *The Selfish Gene*
Thomas Kuhn's *The Structure of Scientific Revolutions*
Geoffrey Parker's *Global Crisis: War, Climate Change and Catastrophe in the Seventeenth Century*
Mathis Wackernagel & William Rees's *Our Ecological Footprint*

SOCIOLOGY

Michelle Alexander's *The New Jim Crow: Mass Incarceration in the Age of Colorblindness*
Gordon Allport's *The Nature of Prejudice*
Albert Bandura's *Aggression: A Social Learning Analysis*
Hanna Batatu's *The Old Social Classes And The Revolutionary Movements Of Iraq*
Ha-Joon Chang's *Kicking Away the Ladder*
W. E. B. Du Bois's *The Souls of Black Folk*
Émile Durkheim's *On Suicide*
Frantz Fanon's *Black Skin, White Masks*
Frantz Fanon's *The Wretched of the Earth*
Eric Foner's *Reconstruction: America's Unfinished Revolution, 1863-1877*
Eugene Genovese's *Roll, Jordan, Roll: The World the Slaves Made*
Jack Goldstone's *Revolution and Rebellion in the Early Modern World*
Antonio Gramsci's *The Prison Notebooks*
Richard Herrnstein & Charles A Murray's *The Bell Curve: Intelligence and Class Structure in American Life*
Eric Hoffer's *The True Believer: Thoughts on the Nature of Mass Movements*
Jane Jacobs's *The Death and Life of Great American Cities*
Robert Lucas's *Why Doesn't Capital Flow from Rich to Poor Countries?*
Jay Macleod's *Ain't No Makin' It: Aspirations and Attainment in a Low Income Neighborhood*
Elaine May's *Homeward Bound: American Families in the Cold War Era*
Douglas McGregor's *The Human Side of Enterprise*
C. Wright Mills's *The Sociological Imagination*

Thomas Piketty's *Capital in the Twenty-First Century*
Robert D. Putman's *Bowling Alone*
David Riesman's *The Lonely Crowd: A Study of the Changing American Character*
Edward Said's *Orientalism*
Joan Wallach Scott's *Gender and the Politics of History*
Theda Skocpol's *States and Social Revolutions*
Max Weber's *The Protestant Ethic and the Spirit of Capitalism*

THEOLOGY

Augustine's *Confessions*
Benedict's *Rule of St Benedict*
Gustavo Gutiérrez's *A Theology of Liberation*
Carole Hillenbrand's *The Crusades: Islamic Perspectives*
David Hume's *Dialogues Concerning Natural Religion*
Immanuel Kant's *Religion within the Boundaries of Mere Reason*
Ernst Kantorowicz's *The King's Two Bodies: A Study in Medieval Political Theology*
Søren Kierkegaard's *The Sickness Unto Death*
C. S. Lewis's *The Abolition of Man*
Saba Mahmood's *The Politics of Piety: The Islamic Revival and the Feminist Subjec*t
Baruch Spinoza's *Ethics*
Keith Thomas's *Religion and the Decline of Magic*

COMING SOON

Chris Argyris's *The Individual and the Organisation*
Seyla Benhabib's *The Rights of Others*
Walter Benjamin's *The Work Of Art in the Age of Mechanical Reproduction*
John Berger's *Ways of Seeing*
Pierre Bourdieu's *Outline of a Theory of Practice*
Mary Douglas's *Purity and Danger*
Roland Dworkin's *Taking Rights Seriously*
James G. March's *Exploration and Exploitation in Organisational Learning*
Ikujiro Nonaka's *A Dynamic Theory of Organizational Knowledge Creation*
Griselda Pollock's *Vision and Difference*
Amartya Sen's *Inequality Re-Examined*
Susan Sontag's *On Photography*
Yasser Tabbaa's *The Transformation of Islamic Art*
Ludwig von Mises's *Theory of Money and Credit*

Printed in the United States
by Baker & Taylor Publisher Services